The Military Veteran Entrepreneur

The Business Journeys of America's Most Successful Military Veteran Founders

By Marcus Gee-Lim & Tim Hsia

Sign up for more news about
Military Veteran Startups and
Military Veteran Founders here:
https://www.contextvc.com/sign-up

Table of Contents

Bill Foley _____ 3
Fred Smith _____ 11
Bob Parsons _____ 24
Ross Perot _____ 38
Phil Knight _____ 56
Chuck Feeney _____ 74
Berry Gordy, Jr. _____ 88
Vincent Viola _____ 100
Sam Walton _____ 108
Jim Kimsey _____ 123
Richard Kinder _____ 135
Gordon Logan _____ 140
Phyllis Newhouse _____ 145
Stephen Schwarzman _____ 154
Charlie Munger _____ 161
Jack Taylor _____ 169
Chuck Wallace _____ 180
Dave Liniger _____ 186

I.

Bill Foley

U.S. Air Force

Fidelity National Finance

William "Bill" P. Foley II was born in Austin, Texas in 1944. His father was an Air Force officer and his mother was a homemaker, and the family moved every few years due to his father's deployments, though they always spent summers in Amarillo, Texas, where his mother's family had roots as ranchers.[1] The family lived in Alaska, California, Virginia, Pennsylvania, Maryland, Venezuela, and Ottawa, the place where Foley (a first-grader at the time) picked up a love for shimmy, an informal style of pickup ice hockey that he remembers where "you'd just try to get the puck and score."[2] His obsession with shimmy as a kid would turn into a lifelong love for ice hockey, ultimately culminating in him bringing a new NHL franchise to Las Vegas – but more on that later.

After finishing high school, Foley followed in his father's footsteps and joined the military. He attended the United States Military Academy at West Point, swimming and competing in lacrosse – and doing a bit of investing. While enrolled as a student, Foley began playing the stock market. "I kept my own charts, did everything by hand," he recalls. "I had a broker in New York City. I'd run down and make a collect phone call. I wasn't very scientific. I got interested in oil. I also invested in a lot of airlines. Regional airlines were getting merged — Mohawk, Bonanza, Air West, Pacific Airlines. I did really well with them. I tried to take my losses quick. I started with $2,000 dad gave me. I ended up with $25,000, which was a lot of money in 1967."[3] Then he lost it all.[4] Aside from monetary lessons, Foley also gained some leadership pointers from his time in school. "West

---

[1] Davis, Noah. "Bill Foley's Big Bet." Worth (blog), October 12, 2016. https://www.worth.com/bill-foleys-big-bet/.
[2] Davis, Noah. "Bill Foley's Big Bet." Worth (blog), October 12, 2016. https://www.worth.com/bill-foleys-big-bet/.
[3] Struckman's Blog. "Montana's Cash Cowboy," January 13, 2012. https://struckman.wordpress.com/2012/01/13/montanas-cash-cowboy/.
[4] Ramkumar, Amrith. "Billionaire Bill Foley Is SPAC Market's Overlooked Star." *Wall Street Journal*, April 4, 2021, sec. Markets. https://www.wsj.com/articles/billionaire-bill-foley-is-spac-markets-overlooked-star-11617537600.

Point taught me that you look to your mission first, your men, and then yourself," he recalls. "That's what I believe really helped create the businessman that I became over the years".[5] Foley graduated with the class of 1967 with a degree in engineering.[6]

After graduating, he joined the Air Force, taking advantage of a West Point policy that allowed graduates to join their father's branch of service instead of the Army. While he'd always wanted to be a pilot as a kid, Foley's eyesight kept him from getting his wings. Instead, he took a position as an Air Force liaison at Boeing in Seattle, as part of the Air Force Plant Representative Office.[7] "I started off as an industrial engineer—I had a really good engineering background—and eventually I became a development engineer, so I was working on all these terrific Boeing programs like the short range attack missile, which was the precursor to the cruise missile, Minuteman III, and Burner II—a second stage spy satellite booster rocket," he recalls. "Eventually I became a contracting officer because I helped save the government a lot of money. By the time I left as a captain after four years, I had personal authority to sign a contract up to a billion dollars. I was about twenty five years old at the time."[8] At the same time he was saving money for the government, Foley was also investing in himself, earning an MBA from Seattle University in 1970 and also finding a life partner –

---

[5] "From West Point to Wine: Bill Foley's Principles for Building a Legacy." Accessed March 23, 2023.
https://www.cnbc.com/advertorial/2021/06/29/from-west-point-to-wine-bill-foleys-principles-for-building-a-legacy.html.

[6] "Mention 'Army' and Golden Knights' Bill Foley Beams with Pride | Las Vegas Review-Journal." Accessed March 23, 2023.
https://www.reviewjournal.com/sports/sports-columns/ed-graney/mention-army-and-golden-knights-bill-foley-beams-with-pride-1928091/.

[7] Davis, Noah. "Bill Foley's Big Bet." *Worth* (blog), October 12, 2016.
https://www.worth.com/bill-foleys-big-bet/.

[8] K&L Wines On the Trail Blog. "On the Trail with Bill Foley," November 6, 2017.
https://onthetrail.klwines.com/on-the-trail-blog/2017/11/5/on-the-trail-with-bill-foley.

his wife Carol, a flight attendant he'd met at a party and married before he left the Air Force.[9]

Having mastered engineering and earning his Master's in Business Administration, Foley turned his sights to learning law post-Air Force. He attended law school at the University of Washington, funded by his wife's paychecks. "I had an uncle who was a lawyer and I had admired his career," he recalls, "plus I wanted to learn a different way of thinking. I was an engineer as an undergrad and I got a masters in business at night while I was in the service, but I wanted that different thought process that you get from being a lawyer, using the Socratic method when you go to class."[10] He succeeded in his new environment, earning his J.D. in 1974 before quickly finding work as a corporate lawyer.

Foley's law work took him to Arizona the same year he graduated to work for Phoenix-based Streich, Lang, Weeks, Cardon & French. He worked at the firm for two years before establishing his own firm, Foley, Clark & Nye, in 1976. While doing legal work for a local savings & loan company, he helped his client acquire a small title insurance company named Fidelity National Financial (FNF) in 1980.[11] Title insurance is basically insurance for people or entities that own property, shielding those who hold the titles of real estate properties from losing money due to claims against the property – a key piece of protection for businesses and landowners. While he continued working at the law firm, he paid attention to FNF's growth, and saw its revenues rapidly increase from $6 million to $40 million

---

[9] Kramer, Joe. "Countdown to Puck Drop - Day 67 - Bill Foley's Journey from Black Knight to Golden Knight." The Hockey Writers, July 27, 2019.
https://thehockeywriters.com/countdown-puck-drop-golden-knights-bill-foley-journey/.

[10] K&L Wines On the Trail Blog. "On the Trail with Bill Foley," November 6, 2017.
https://onthetrail.klwines.com/on-the-trail-blog/2017/11/5/on-the-trail-with-bill-foley.

[11] "William P. Foley II 1944— Biography - The Deal Maker, Key Business and Leadership Strategies." Accessed March 25, 2023.
https://www.referenceforbusiness.com/biography/F-L/Foley-William-P-II-1944.html.

over the next few years.[12] In 1984, he organized a purchase of FNF with a few other investors, signaling the end of his career in law and the beginning of an eventual business empire.

"I moved away from law when I did a leveraged buyout of a small title insurance firm back in 1984 and that was the basis of our public companies today," he remembers. "I think we paid twenty-one million—we borrowed seventeen million and we put down about four million. I owned about 51%; I begged and borrowed all the money to make the investment. I got it from my family, we put a mortgage on our house, whatever we could do to raise money, we did it. That group of businesses today now has a market value of about sixty-two billion."[13]

After gaining control of the business, Foley soon began rapidly expanding FNF using the business' relatively large cash flow due to its high return on equity to invest in expanding its operations. He put money into acquiring independent insurance agencies in order to better control distribution of policies, and also bought into regional title insurance firms in order to expand his business geographically. In 1987, FNF acquired Western Title Insurance Company, granting it a large presence in California overnight.[14] It went public the same year, granting investing-minded Foley an even larger pool of capital to work with. In 1992, the same year FNF began being traded on the New York Stock Exchange, the company gobbled up Meridian Title Insurance Company, expanding its operations into Florida and much of the rest of the eastern U.S.[15] Just eight years later, in

---

[12] "William P. Foley II 1944— Biography - The Deal Maker, Key Business and Leadership Strategies." Accessed March 25, 2023.
https://www.referenceforbusiness.com/biography/F-L/Foley-William-P-II-1944.html.
[13] K&L Wines On the Trail Blog. "On the Trail with Bill Foley," November 6, 2017.
https://onthetrail.klwines.com/on-the-trail-blog/2017/11/5/on-the-trail-with-bill-foley.
[14] "Company Profile." Accessed March 24, 2023.
https://interactive.web.insurance.ca.gov/companyprofile/companyprofile?event=companyProfile&doFunction=getCompanyProfile&eid=5931.
[15] "Fidelity National Title Insurance Company." Accessed March 25, 2023. https://www.fntic.com/aboutus.aspx.

2000, FNF became the largest title insurance company in the U.S. with its purchase of Chicago Title Corporation, the second-largest title insurer at the time.[16]

At the same time he was solidifying FNF's position at the top of the title insurance market, Foley was also investing in other companies and spinning off new businesses. The company invested so much in software in the 1990s that Foley was able to create Fidelity National Information Services, which develops software used by 95% of the world's largest banks.[17] He began investing in struggling companies using FNF's substantial cash flow, rehabilitating companies with strong fundamentals that struggled with management issues. A self-described "dictator," Foley makes frequent slashes to management of the companies he invests in.[18] That way, he says,"if there's a failure, it's my fault."[19] He also gave a boost to a failing Carl's Jr. by fixing its management issues and combining it with other chains under the same parent company – though he had to drop the business after a few down years.[20] By the early 2000s, Foley had a hand in multiple insurance markets, many different software companies,

---

[16] "Fidelity National Title Insurance Company." Accessed March 25, 2023. https://www.fntic.com/aboutus.aspx.

[17] FIS Global. "Large Financial Institutions | FIS." Accessed March 25, 2023. https://www.fisglobal.com/en/financial-institutions/large-financial-institutions.

[18] "Bournemouth Takeover: New Owner Bill Foley 'a Dictator' and 'Needs to Be Captain of the Ship' - BBC Sport." Accessed March 25, 2023. https://www.bbc.com/sport/football/63982991.

[19] Street Journal, Richard Gibson Staff Reporter of The Wall. "Bill Foley Built an Empire By Buying Ailing Also-Rans." *Wall Street Journal*, December 2, 1998, sec. Front Section. https://www.wsj.com/articles/SB912553501104864000.

[20] Street Journal, Richard Gibson Staff Reporter of The Wall. "Bill Foley Built an Empire By Buying Ailing Also-Rans." Wall Street Journal, December 2, 1998, sec. Front Section. https://www.wsj.com/articles/SB912553501104864000.

a Pacific Northwest timber company, and various California wineries.[21]

More recently, Foley has tried his hand at sports while spinning off his investments into separate companies. Foley currently sits as the chairman of FNF (of course) and Cannae Holdings (which houses many of Foley's operating companies). In 2016, he became the lead investor in the latest NHL expansion team, creating the Las Vegas Golden Knights under the banner of Black Knight Sports & Entertainment. This, of course, only came about after a period of analysis – "We did a market study for Las Vegas and determined that we had about 200,000 avid hockey fans, people from Minnesota or Canada, the northeast. People trying to get to a nice climate. We went to the high end and our average ticket price is about $88. The league average is down in the $70s. Financially, we will be strong," he claims.[22] He's also invested in other sports teams. The Henderson Silver Knights act as the Golden Knights' development team, the Vegas Knight Hawks are his foray into indoor football (the American kind), and he's also recently bought into soccer teams overseas, purchasing ownership of AFC Bournemouth in the Premier League and FC Lorient in France's Ligue 1.[23]

Lately, it seems, Foley also focused on something else he enjoys – winemaking. He's invested in a large number of California wineries, though of course the investments only came about when it made financial sense to do so. "The recession hit and I bought properties that were a little distressed and there

---

[21] Struckman's Blog. "Montana's Cash Cowboy," January 13, 2012. https://struckman.wordpress.com/2012/01/13/montanas-cash-cowboy/.

[22] Ewing, Mark. "Bill Foley And The National Hockey League's Newest Franchise, The Vegas Golden Knights." Forbes. Accessed March 25, 2023. https://www.forbes.com/sites/markewing/2017/07/16/bill-foley-and-the-national-hockey-leagues-newest-franchise-the-vegas-golden-knights/.

[23] France 24. "Bournemouth Owner Bill Foley Buys Stake in French Club Lorient," January 13, 2023. https://www.france24.com/en/live-news/20230113-bournemouth-owner-bill-foley-buys-stake-in-french-club-lorient.

was a value proposition," he says. "I was convinced that by the time we got to 2012 or '13 we would be in hyper-inflation. Didn't happen. But I ended up buying a lot of properties from people who got over-extended, then over-levered. I would come in, do about 25 percent leverage and 75 percent equity so there would never be an issue about valuations. Since that time, these properties have gone through the roof, they've really gotten valuable. Cabernet land in Alexander Valley…I was buying it for $50,000 an acre three years ago. Today it's $150,000 an acre."[24]

Over the course of his investing career so far, Foley has come up with a clear, winning formula that's seen him consistently (and meaningfully) outperform the S&P 500. He's positioned his companies to compete at their best within their markets, has made shrewd investments in struggling companies at the perfect time, and has shown a knack for slimming down waste and ineffective management. He's also shown a true love for the game, continuing to invest in new markets to this day.

---

[24] Ewing, Mark. "Bill Foley And The National Hockey League's Newest Franchise, The Vegas Golden Knights." Forbes. Accessed March 25, 2023.
https://www.forbes.com/sites/markewing/2017/07/16/bill-foley-and-the-national-hockey-leagues-newest-franchise-the-vegas-golden-knights/.

II.

Fred Smith

U.S. Marines

FedEx

Fred Smith was born Frederick Wallace Smith to James Frederick "Fred" Smith and Sally Wallace in Marks, Mississippi on August 11, 1944. Named after his father, Fred had one brother and two sisters.[25] His family was quite well-off; his father was a successful businessman who founded both the Smith Motor Coach Company (a bus company) and the Toddle House restaurant chain, which he ran with the help of Fred's older brother Gary. The Smith Motor Coach Company was eventually bought out by and incorporated into the Greyhound Corporation, while the restaurant chain quickly grew, serving over 200 locations in almost 90 cities in the southeast at the peak of its business.[26]

Although money was far from an issue for the Smiths thanks to the senior Fred's business successes, tragedy struck when the younger Fred was only 4: his father died, leaving behind a wife and four children to fend for themselves. Fred Senior had amassed a fortune of $17 million by the time he passed. As a result, Smith was raised by his mother and uncles for most of his childhood. Adding to Smith's trials as a young boy, he was diagnosed with Legg-Calvé-Perthes syndrome, a bone disease which limited his mobility as a child.[27] Luckily, Smith recovered by age 10, becoming an avid football player and even an amateur pilot by age 15. His flying skills were nurtured under the guidance of Colonel Fred Hook, a Memphis Air Force officer he met at a National Guard Conference in Nashville who would eventually become his stepfather.

---

[25] "Fred Smith 1944— Biography - Early Life, The Road to Fedex," accessed March 10, 2022,
https://www.referenceforbusiness.com/biography/S-Z/Smith-Fred-1944.html.

[26] Bob Greene, "Waffles and FedEx: An American Tale," CNN, August 11, 2013,
https://www.cnn.com/2013/08/11/opinion/greene-waffle-fedex/index.html.

[27] "10 Things You Didn't Know About Fred Smith," US News & World Report, accessed March 11, 2022,
//www.usnews.com/news/campaign-2008/articles/2008/07/24/10-things-you-didnt-know-about-fred-smith.

He attended private schools in Memphis for his early schooling, becoming class president at Memphis University School, a college prep school, in his senior year while participating in a variety of sports and working as sports editor of the school's newspaper. According to his sister, he was destined for business greatness even as a teenager, following in his late father's footsteps: "If you met Fred then, you would have been dazzled by him. This man was charming, articulate, and just winning. You could follow him anywhere as a leader. He would start waving his hands around, and conjure up these images, and your checkbook just bounces in your hand, and you are ready to follow him over the next hill, and wherever. He was a terrific salesman, who made fantasies come alive."[28] His success in high school led to his acceptance into Yale for a bachelor's degree in economics.

Throughout his early life, Smith never doubted that he would join the military. Many of his close male relatives had fought for the U.S. military in various wars before him, and Smith had no plans to break that tradition. His Uncle Sam had fought in the European theater during the second World War, while his uncles Arthur and Bill served in the Pacific. His father was a Navy Commander during the war as well, and his stepfather was a fighter pilot in China who married Smith's mother after retiring from the Air Force. Even his eventual father-in-law served as a marine in both World War Two and the Korean War.

Following in his family's footsteps, Fred's only question about service after graduating high school was which branch of the military he would choose. While he originally wanted to become a naval aviator, Smith was unable to follow through with his dreams of flying for his country after he failed to meet the Navy's eyesight standard for pilots. Putting his powers of youth to work, Smith made a decision: he would serve with the Marines. Why? He liked their uniforms, and the platoon leaders

---

[28] Vance Trimble, *Overnight Success: Federal Express And: Frederick Smith, Its Renegade Creator*, 1st edition (New York: Crown, 1993).

course (PLC) took place during the summer, allowing him to participate in athletics and social events freely during the academic year at Yale.[29]

In 1962, Smith started his time at Yale, where he would eventually earn his bachelor's in economics. There, he struggled to balance school, his passion for flying, and his other passions. He failed to make the football team and saw his grades suffer before one pivotal incident during the summer of 1963. While home from school, Fred crashed his new Corvette while driving with a friend named Mike Gadberry. According to one spectator, "The car was bouncing end over end. It was bouncing high in the air … For the car to act like that, it had to be running seventy-five, eighty, even one hundred miles an hour. The car was upside down several hundred feet on down the highway."[30] While Fred survived the accident, his friend was not so fortunate. Mike died at the site of the crash, while Fred was sent to the hospital for concussion and shock. One of Smith's close friends at the time noted the accident's impact on Fred's outlook on life: "I think that he felt very badly, and I think he pushed himself to the limit in everything he did."

After the crash, his newfound determination to live his life to its fullest set him back on the path to success. Smith eventually became president of the Delta Kappa Epsilon (DKE) fraternity and joined the secretive Skull and Bones society, a selective group which only accepted the most elite student leaders on campus. During his tenure with these organizations, he rubbed shoulders with other leaders-to-be: one of his friends and fraternity brothers at DKE was future president George W. Bush, and Smith was also close friends with future Secretary of State John Kerry. Smith also continued his romance with the skies, revitalizing the Yale Flying Club by recruiting members and securing a deal with the Piper Aircraft Company to lease the club planes.

---

[29] U.S. Army G-4, *BATTLEFIELD TO BOARDROOM FULL PROGRAM*, 2014, https://www.youtube.com/watch?v=_QeZ2A5bN1s.
[30] Vance Trimble, *Overnight Success: Federal Express And: Frederick Smith, Its Renegade Creator*, 1st edition (New York: Crown, 1993).

In 1965, one of the most fabled and retold events of Fred's life took place. As part of his coursework for an economics class, he was tasked with writing a term paper on the process of transporting goods in the U.S. When he looked at the direction that society was taking at the time, Smith hypothesized that developments in computer technology led by firms like IBM would lead to a "computerized society" where companies operating with increased informational power would require goods to be moved around faster than currently possible. One way to move goods more efficiently, Smith wrote, was to move away from transporting goods with a focus on movement from point A to point B.

Smith describes it best himself: "The solution was, in my mind, to have an integrated air and ground system, which had never been done. And to operate not on a linear basis, where you try to take things from one point to another, but operate in a systematic manner. Sort of the way a bank clearing house does … They have a bank clearing house in the middle of all the banks and everybody sends someone down there and they swap everything around. Well, that had been done in transportation before: the Indian post office, the French post office. American Airlines had tried a system like that shortly after World War II. But the demand side and supply side had really not met at an appropriate level of maturation."[31] His paper failed to touch on the specifics of how such a system would operate, and just earned him a "gentlemanly C."[32] The idea Smith wrote in the paper would eventually become the concept behind FedEx's overnight express system.

As Fred wrapped up his time at Yale, the U.S. ramped up its involvement in Vietnam. Troop levels had increased tenfold since his freshman year, and Fred figured he was headed across the globe after he graduated. He'd had brief

---

[31] "Frederick W. Smith | Academy of Achievement," accessed March 11, 2022, https://achievement.org/achiever/frederick-w-smith/#interview.
[32] Eugene Linden, "Frederick W. Smith Of Federal Express: He Didn't Get There Overnight," Inc.com, April 1, 1984, https://www.inc.com/magazine/19840401/8479.html.

thoughts of attending grad school, but he decided that that path was not for him. Instead, he made his way to Quantico, Virginia for training. The usual nine-month basic training was compacted into just five months, with training six days a week plus nights. After completing basic training, the Navy sent Fred to the Defense Language school in Monterey, California. On completing his "training" in Monterey (Smith confessed that he didn't learn much Vietnamese there, but became well acquainted with the geography of Northern California and "all the spots that were good to go for a sloe gin fizz"), he was sent overseas to meet with his unit.[33]

While Fred was originally assigned to the 3rd Marine Division, he was switched to 1st Marine Division at Okinawa, joining the division shortly after Operation Union 2 in 1967. Once he settled into his role there, Smith rose through the ranks, becoming a Platoon Leader, serving with India and Lima Companies, and also briefly becoming an 81mm Mortar Platoon Leader. He was slated for promotion to become an S-4 logistics officer, but he was shifted from this path due to a shortage of officers. His PLC training pushed him to the front of the line, and Smith became Commanding Officer of K Company, 3rd Battalion, 5th Marines.[34]

His time with the Marines saw him serving on the front lines. He was assigned to an area just 200 miles south of the demilitarized zone dividing the North and South, which saw over 5,000 Marines killed by 1967. His experiences in combat led to several close calls: in one instance, a bullet severed the chin strap of his helmet without harming him. In another incident, an ambush by enemy soldiers killed the men directly in front of, beside, and behind Smith. By the end of his first tour, Fred had seen much of the horrors of war and its effects on the people

---

[33] U.S. Army G-4, *BATTLEFIELD TO BOARDROOM FULL PROGRAM*, 2014, https://www.youtube.com/watch?v=QeZ2A5bN1s.
[34] "Vietnam Experience Inspires Veteran to Create Overnight Delivery Company," www.army.mil, accessed March 7, 2022, https://www.army.mil/article/121066/vietnam_experience_inspires_veteran_to_create_overnight_delivery_company.

serving next to him, but he emerged with only a few wounds: his list of minor injuries included a small piece of shrapnel to the eye and another lodged in his back.

After returning home from his first tour, Fred quickly decided to head back to Vietnam for a second tour. This time, he served as a general's aide before moving on as a forward air controller with Marine Observation Squadron 2 at Marble Mountain, partially fulfilling his dream of serving his country from the air. He flew over 200 missions during his service in the skies before eventually returning home and being discharged in 1969. He left the Marines with a Silver Star, a Bronze Star, and two Purple Hearts, along with the Presidential Regiment Citation and the Navy Commendation Medal.[35]

Many of Smith's most important lessons were learned in Vietnam. Out of college, Fred was a very privileged young man: he'd received leadership training, attended Yale, and had gone to only private schools throughout his life. His family was well off, and his bubble of money and elite institutions largely prevented him from interacting with blue-collar, working families. In Vietnam, though, the working class were his comrades in arms. There, Smith served side by side with them, and he credits his time in Vietnam with giving him more insight into the minds of workers compared to other executives in senior management after the war.

Besides learning about how to talk to and lead the people who make militaries (and multibillion dollar corporations) run, Smith also learned a thing or two about the necessity of organization and logistics in his time with the military. The Marines' tight air-ground coordination and other joint operations showed him the power of cooperation, providing him a template for Fedex's future air-ground integration, which saw delivery staff organized like pilots. According to Smith, "The organizational disciplines that militaries have developed over centuries are at the heart of all organized activity in the world. If

---

[35] "Frederick Smith - Recipient -," accessed April 14, 2022, http://valor.militarytimes.com/hero/23898.

you brought Julius Caesar back to Earth, he would understand the organization of Fedex because he basically invented it ...One of the first things the Romans did that lead to their power was to focus on logistics [and] build an unprecedented communications network in a series of roads. All major organizations are built on the same principles and organizational structure that [the U.S. Military] deals with every day."[36]

By the time Fred left the service, it was becoming clear to him that the computerized society he'd predicted in his economics term paper all the way back in Yale was, in fact, coming to be. At just 25 years of age when he left the Marines, Smith was still filled with both naivete and ambition. Using his family's considerable wealth, Smith purchased a controlling interest in Ark Aviation Sales, an aircraft maintenance company, in 1970. His stepfather, Colonel Hook, had purchased a 50% stake in the company in 1965, but the business was on a downturn until Fred stepped in. He pivoted the company to trading used jets and jet parts, which would eventually net him a fleet of 14 planes by the time he founded Federal Express in 1971. Ark Aviation earned $9 million during the first two years after Fred purchased it, and the business began to turn a profit.[37]

To start his larger endeavor, Smith needed both customers and money. After sifting through a handful of ideas, Fred approached the Federal Reserve with a proposal: he would use his small fleet of jets to expedite the movement of the Fed's check-clearing services. At the time, the bank was responsible for clearing checks between banks in major cities across the U.S. The paper checks had to be physically moved across the country between banks before they could clear, a pain point for both customers and the Fed. Smith proposed implementing the centralized shipping system he'd outlined in his Yale paper, and the Fed Board seemed to be interested in his idea: checks would be picked up from cities by plane, brought to a central location

---

[36] U.S. Army G-4, *BATTLEFIELD TO BOARDROOM FULL PROGRAM*, 2014, https://www.youtube.com/watch?v=_QeZ2A5bN1s.
[37] Vance Trimble, *Overnight Success: Federal Express And: Frederick Smith, Its Renegade Creator*, 1st edition (New York: Crown, 1993).

for sorting, and sent out to their proper destinations overnight. Fred officially incorporated the company, then named the Federal Express Corporation, on June 18, 1971, and invested $3.6 million of his father's money to purchase two jets in anticipation of his partnership with the Fed, but the bank backed out of the deal last-minute due to internal politics.

Relatively unfazed, Fred pushed ahead with his plans for the newly official company, securing eight used jets to increase his fleet's size to 10. To fund buying the jets as well as the costs of his future operations, Fred enlisted the help of Wall Street banking firm White, Weld & Company. The company linked Fred with two market research firms (who performed their research without knowledge of the other firm) in order to prove the viability of the business to potential investors. The firms concluded that establishing the company would require a fleet of 30 jets and between $6 million and $15 million (excluding the costs of the jets). This would mean moving 1.6 million packages per year, roughly 1% of all of the domestic air shipping market at the time. Using this research, Fred turned to White, Weld & Company, who promised to help him raise $15-$30 million from investors in order to start the company.

In early 1972, the business was ready to dip its toes into operation. Fred purchased six USPS contracts for five nightly flights per week in the Midwest in order to show possible investors proof of concept. To fund operations with no investors at the time, he invested another $2 million from his father's trust fund. At the end of 1972, after a year of operations, the results of Federal Express's test run were in: the company finished out the year with $2.8 million in income, but expenses of $3.7 million.[38] Income came from an even split of airmail contracts and odd charter work. The company was running at operational costs of $1 million a year, and Fred Smith saw that changes needed to be made. He doubled down on his formula, investing more in the business with a focus on expanding his pilot base. He opened the

---

[38] Vance Trimble, *Overnight Success: Federal Express And: Frederick Smith, Its Renegade Creator*, 1st edition (New York: Crown, 1993).

Federal Express Training School to train ex-military pilots, with 273 pilots passing the program after a year. Fred saw that operating on a small scale would never pull in investors, and that a national network would be needed to entice new clients. According to analysis, Memphis would be the most economical location for a central sorting facility for his national expansion, so the company purchased a facility there.[39] Fred also bought out the engineering company working on the Federal Express jets as they were worried about the Express never paying off the debts owed for work on the planes. By March of 1973, the company had a fleet of nine jets, a new center in Memphis, and 150 employees. All of this expansion for the future with little to show in the way of profit put the company in dire straits - Federal Express was fully broke, and needed $1.5 million to keep operating. To make this up, Fred took out a $2 million loan from Union National Bank, leveraging a block of stock from his father's trust company which did not actually exist, literally committing commercial fraud to keep his company afloat.

Using the newly-expanded company resources, Federal Express grew its operations to more major cities, including St. Louis, Dallas, Kansas City, Atlanta, and Nashville. Following this expansion, the company's first air express service flight took place on March 12, 1973. The flight landed at the company's Memphis hub with a grand total of just six packages, including a birthday present for Smith and a package from a company salesman. As this was obviously not the most satisfactory showing, the company took a step back for a month to expand before another flight on April 17, 1973. This time, the company moved 186 packages on 14 different planes.[40] To fund this expansion, though, the company fell even deeper into the red. Smith eventually had to take out a massive loan of $23.5 million from General Dynamics, with a repayment period of just four months and an option for General Dynamics to buy 80.1% of

---

[39] "FedEx History," FedEx, accessed March 31, 2022, https://www.fedex.com/en-us/about/history.html.
[40] "FedEx History," FedEx, accessed March 31, 2022, https://www.fedex.com/en-us/about/history.html.

Federal Express stock for $16 million.[41] Even if the company didn't bite on their option, the Express would still have to hand over 6% of its stock. While Smith obviously did not want to hand over control of the company like this, the money was necessary for much-needed expansions, so he accepted.

During this early struggle to keep the company afloat while also expanding operations, another of Fred Smith's legendary stories took place. At one point, the company had just $5,000 left to operate with while working out their agreement with General Dynamics. While traveling for company business, Smith saw a flight to Las Vegas and shifted his itinerary on a whim. There, he gambled to keep his company afloat. "I was very committed to the people that had signed on with me, and if we were going to go down, we were going to go down with a fight," Smith reflected on the trip, "It wasn't going to be because I checked out and didn't finish."[42] He ended up turning a few hundred dollars into $27,000, helping keep employees paid and planes fueled until the loan came through.

After Smith won in Vegas, things began to look up. While the company still had budgeting issues, General Dynamics extended their loan period beyond four months, and the Express secured another $23 million loan from a group of banks in October of 1973. The company continued to grow, receiving more rounds of funding later in 1974, but Smith's position at the head of the company was soon called into question. The banking consortium wanted to replace Smith with a CEO who had more commercial experience, and soon after, Smith was called into in 1975 court for the commercial fraud he'd committed to obtain a $2 million loan in 1973.[43] At this point, the company was $49

---

[41] Vance Trimble, *Overnight Success: Federal Express And: Frederick Smith, Its Renegade Creator*, 1st edition (New York: Crown, 1993).
[42] Ann Schmidt, "How Fred Smith Rescued FedEx from Bankruptcy by Playing Blackjack in Las Vegas," Text.Article, FOXBusiness (Fox Business, July 16, 2020), https://www.foxbusiness.com/money/fred-smith-fedex-blackjack-winning-formula.
[43] Vance Trimble, *Overnight Success: Federal Express And: Frederick Smith, Its Renegade Creator*, 1st edition (New York: Crown, 1993).

million in the hole, and had lost over $11 million in the previous fiscal year. In 1976, after Smith was declared not guilty by the jury, the company turned its first annual profit of $3.6 million as it continued to expand its shipping operations, shipping 19,000 parcels per day.[44]

As the company continued to operate in the black the following years, Smith saw his idea come to fruition. However, he knew that the company could grow even more, and that one thing holding it back was the size of the aircrafts it operated. The company became one of the loudest voices in pushing for deregulation of commercial aircraft, eventually leading to the passage of a 1977 bill allowing large planes such as Boeing 727s to be used for shipping purposes.[45] Further government deregulation of shipping helped the company expand even more as the federal government cut down on regulations for interstate shipping in 1980, allowing Federal Express to work even more efficiently.[46] The country was beginning to buy into Smith's idea that a faster, more efficient shipping network was necessary to grow with the times.

Over the next few decades, the Federal Express truly began to take off, both financially and operationally. On April 12, 1978, the company went public, offering 783,000 shares at $24 apiece.[47] In 1979, the company debuted its tracking service named COSMOS (Customers, Operations and Services Master Online System), utilizing early computers and scanning wands to

---

[44] Maggie Zhang, "The Founder Of FedEx Saved The Company From Bankruptcy With His Blackjack Winnings," Business Insider, accessed March 27, 2022,
https://www.businessinsider.com/fedex-saved-from-bankruptcy-with-blackjack-winnings-2014-7.
[45] "FedEx History," FedEx, accessed March 31, 2022,
https://www.fedex.com/en-us/about/history.html.
[46] "Online Extra: Fred Smith on the Birth of FedEx," *Bloomberg.Com*, September 20, 2004,
https://www.bloomberg.com/news/articles/2004-09-19/online-extra-fred-smith-on-the-birth-of-fedex.
[47] "Investor FAQs | FedEx," accessed April 2, 2022,
https://investors.fedex.com/shareowner-services/investor-faqs/default.aspx.

help the business and its customers track their packages. In 1983, it reported $1 billion in revenues, becoming the first company to hit the $1 billion mark within 10 years without mergers or acquisitions.[48] In 1994, Federal Express changed its name to longtime nickname "FedEx" for marketing purposes. By 1995, FedEx had expanded across Europe and Asia, and became the first U.S.-based cargo company with aviation rights in China after its purchase of Evergreen Air.[49] Today, thanks to Smith's early and unwavering vision for the company as well as his foresight, FedEx is the largest transportation and logistics company in the world, valued at over $93 billion.[50, 51]

---

[48] "FedEx History," FedEx, accessed March 31, 2022, https://www.fedex.com/en-us/about/history.html.
[49] "FEDEX TO TAKE OVER EVERGREEN AIR'S ALL-CARGO ROUTE RIGHTS TO CHINA | JOC.Com," accessed April 2, 2022, https://www.joc.com/fedex-take-over-evergreen-airs-all-cargo-route-rights-china_19950226.html.
[50] Kevin Dowd, "Forbes Global 2000: The World's Largest Transportation Companies," Forbes, accessed April 2, 2022, https://www.forbes.com/sites/kevindowd/2021/05/13/forbes-global-2000-the-worlds-largest-transportation-companies/.
[51] "FedEx Corporation (FDX) Valuation Measures & Financial Statistics," accessed April 2, 2022, https://finance.yahoo.com/quote/FDX/key-statistics/.

III.

Bob Parsons

U.S. Marines

GoDaddy

Before becoming a billionaire with businesses in a vast range of fields, from web hosting to golf clubs to motorcycle dealerships, Bob Parsons grew up "as dirt poor as a church rat" in inner-city Baltimore, Maryland.[52] Born to two hardcore gamblers on November 27, 1950, Parsons' family constantly struggled for money as he grew up. His father worked as a furniture salesman, while his mother kept the house. The family of five had little money even without his parents' gambling. "Cards, horses, bingo—you name it. You don't have a lot of money if you're a gambler, particularly if you don't start with lots of it," Parsons remembers.[53] To get himself the things he wanted from a young age, Parsons made money however he could: one story includes a young Parsons buying out a newspaper vending machine before rush hour and selling the papers to commuters at marked-up prices in order to buy a baseball glove.[54]

Although he was clever with money making schemes outside the classroom, Parsons struggled behind a desk. He would have had to repeat the fifth grade if not for an administration error, and as a senior in high school he "was failing most subjects except for gym and lunch."[55] Recounting his senior year in one interview, he touched on both his lack of academic commitment as well as his entry into the military: "I had two friends of mine approach me in the locker room one day

---

[52] "StartupJournal | Worthwhile," June 30, 2006, http://web.archive.org/web/20060630092721/http://www.startupjournal.com/runbusiness/worthwhile/20051207-worthwhile3.html?refresh=on.
[53] Monte Burke, "GoDaddy Billionaire Founder Bob Parsons On His Passion For Golf And Motorcycles," Forbes, accessed April 1, 2022, https://www.forbes.com/sites/monteburke/2017/10/18/godaddy-billionaire-founder-bob-parsons-on-his-passion-for-golf-and-motorcycles/.
[54] Monte Burke, "GoDaddy Billionaire Founder Bob Parsons On His Passion For Golf And Motorcycles," Forbes, accessed April 1, 2022, https://www.forbes.com/sites/monteburke/2017/10/18/godaddy-billionaire-founder-bob-parsons-on-his-passion-for-golf-and-motorcycles/.
[55] bunkered.co.uk, "Meet Bob Parsons: War Vet, Dot-Com Billionaire, Golf...," text/html, bunkered.co.uk (bunkered.co.uk, October 7, 2017), https://www.bunkered.co.uk/, https://www.bunkered.co.uk/golf-news/meet-bob-parsons-war-vet-dot-com-billionaire-pxg-owner.

after gym," he recalls. "They asked me, 'Hey Robert, whatcha gonna do when we're finished high school?' I said, 'I'll probably still be here'. They said, 'Well, we're going to talk to a recruiter from the U.S. Marine Corp. Why don't you come down with us?'"[56] Having no other plans for his future and wanting to avoid repeating his senior year, Parsons followed his friends into the recruiter's office. There, he made one of the most important decisions in his life, enlisting in August of 1968.

After graduating from high school, Parsons and one of his high school friends headed to Parris Island for training. After six months of Marine Corps rifleman training there, Parsons was shipped off to Vietnam to serve with Company D, 1st Battalion, 26th Marine Regiment near Quang Nam province.[57] There, he was tasked with protecting the rice fields which fed the South Vietnamese army, which meant waiting in ambush almost every night.[58] On his first night in Vietnam, Parsons learned that, a few days prior to his arrival, his squad had suffered five casualties, four of which were fatal (among those the most senior men in his squad), and he was called in from South Carolina as one of their replacements. The most senior member of his squad was a 19-year old who had been in Vietnam for just six weeks before Parson's arrival. Before this experience, Parsons had considered himself a nonconformist and a "knucklehead," not dedicating himself to school or anything else, really, but the harsh reality of

---

[56] bunkered.co.uk, "Meet Bob Parsons: War Vet, Dot-Com Billionaire, Golf...," text/html, bunkered.co.uk (bunkered.co.uk, October 7, 2017), https://www.bunkered.co.uk/, https://www.bunkered.co.uk/golf-news/meet-bob-parsons-war-vet-dot-com-billionaire-pxg-owner.

[57] David Andersen and Lameen Witter News Marine Corps, "Former Marine, GoDaddy CEO Talks About His Rise to Success," Military.com, April 10, 2019, https://www.military.com/veteran-jobs/career-advice/military-transition/veteran-ceo-of-go-daddy.html.

[58] "Bob Parsons' Marine Corps Birthday & Veterans Day Salute 2021," Bob Parsons, November 2, 2021, https://bobparsons.com/bob-parsons-marine-corps-birthday-veterans-day-salute-2021/.

Vietnam sobered him up quickly.[59] He recalls asking himself, "How in the world was I going to survive there 13 months when the guy who has been there the longest had been there only six weeks? The other guys had left in bags or on stretchers. It was crazy."[60]

The danger of Vietnam elicited a visceral response in Parsons, changing his outlook on life quickly. Reflecting on how his mindset changed in Vietnam, he recalls: "My thoughts slowly shifted from, 'How am I going to survive?' to 'This is where I'm going to die.' I eventually accepted the worst outcome as inevitable, and when I accepted what was my probable fate, I relaxed, felt at peace, the darkness let go of me, and I was able to think ... Then I made myself two promises: First, I would do everything I could to do my job as a U.S. Marine. Second, I'd do what I could to be alive for the next morning's mail call ...What initially seemed like an overwhelming situation became something I could deal with."[61]

Using his new mindset, Parsons managed to survive the traumatizing violence of Quang Nam for a month, with fellow squadmates suffering grisly injuries almost every day. Eventually, though, the nightly ambushes and patrols found Parsons injured too: While he walked as second point through a village one night, the point man stepped over and missed a tripwire. Parsons wasn't so lucky, tripping the trap and receiving

---

[59] Dan O'Neill, "The Marines 'Totally' Turned Around Bob Parsons and He Won't Stop Paying That Forward," Morning Read, accessed April 4, 2022, https://www.si.com/golf/news/the-marines-turned-around-bob-parsons-and-hell-never-stop-paying-that-forward.

[60] Dan O'Neill, "The Marines 'Totally' Turned Around Bob Parsons and He Won't Stop Paying That Forward," Morning Read, accessed April 4, 2022, https://www.si.com/golf/news/the-marines-turned-around-bob-parsons-and-hell-never-stop-paying-that-forward.

[61] "Bob Parsons' Marine Corps Birthday & Veterans Day Salute 2021," Bob Parsons, November 2, 2021, https://bobparsons.com/bob-parsons-marine-corps-birthday-veterans-day-salute-2021/.

shrapnel in his elbow and both of his legs from the explosion.[62] Following his injury, Parsons was med-evaced to Japan where he recuperated for two months before finishing out his tour as a Marine Corps Intelligence courier. He returned home with the Combat Action Ribbon, the Vietnam Gallantry Cross, and the Purple Heart.[63]

While he did make it home alive and healed from his shrapnel wounds, all was not well with Parsons mentally. Though he didn't know it at the time, Parsons suffered from post-traumatic stress disorder like many other veterans after his deeply dangerous experiences in Vietnam. "The guy that came home was a very different guy than the guy that left. The guy that came home didn't like being around people, he had a short temper, he was depressed, he buried himself in his work ... I didn't know I had PTSD but I knew I was different," he recalls[64]

After working at a steel mill for six months after coming home to Baltimore, Parsons kicked himself into gear, seizing on a lust for life inspired in part by his experiences in Vietnam. He took a step that high school (and fifth grade) Bob Parsons would never expect: using his veteran's education benefits, he enrolled at the University of Baltimore, choosing to major in accounting. The old Parsons was still lurking inside, though, even with his newfound dedication to education: "I didn't even know you needed a major," he remembers. "I just chose the first one listed

---

[62] "Bob Parsons' Marine Corps Birthday & Veterans Day Salute 2021," Bob Parsons, November 2, 2021,
https://bobparsons.com/bob-parsons-marine-corps-birthday-veterans-day-salute-2021/.

[63] bunkered.co.uk, "Meet Bob Parsons: War Vet, Dot-Com Billionaire, Golf...," text/html, bunkered.co.uk (bunkered.co.uk, October 7, 2017), https://www.bunkered.co.uk/,
https://www.bunkered.co.uk/golf-news/meet-bob-parsons-war-vet-dot-com-billionaire-pxg-owner.

[64] "Coming Home | Bob Parsons - Field Tripping (Podcast)," Listen Notes, accessed April 6, 2022,
https://www.listennotes.com/podcasts/field-tripping/coming-home-bob-parsons-W2eGRhmOEXc/.

in the book."[65] Despite not knowing about the details of higher education, Parsons excelled in school. He graduated magna cum laude in 1975, crediting his time as a Marine with teaching him the discipline needed to tap into his talents and succeed where he previously couldn't: "When I went into the Marine Corps, I was pretty aimless. When I came out, I understood discipline, responsibility, honor. All those things. The Marine Corps taught me that 'pretty clean' is dirty."[66]

Post-graduation, Parsons studied for and easily passed his CPA exam before landing a job at a direct mail company. There, he worked his way to the top. On one work trip out to the San Francisco Bay Area, Parsons was killing time at a bookstore near Stanford University when he came across a book teaching programming in the Basic language. After leafing through the book, Parsons was hooked. "It was a hobby," he recalls, "but I got really good at it."[67] He soon developed an accounting software (which he named MoneyCounts) for his own personal use, and was convinced that he could sell it, thinking, "If it's good enough for me – and my standards are pretty high – then why not sell it?"[68] Thus began his journey into entrepreneurship.

Using the $15,000 he had saved up, Parsons decided to launch a company based on MoneyCounts while still working his day job. Like many other entrepreneurs before him, his first few ventures were duds: "When you go into business for the first

---

[65] "Go Daddy's Bob Parsons Takes His Act to a Bigger Stage - December 1, ...," archive.ph, January 30, 2013, https://archive.ph/SMlCU.
[66] bunkered.co.uk, "Meet Bob Parsons: War Vet, Dot-Com Billionaire, Golf...," text/html, bunkered.co.uk (bunkered.co.uk, October 7, 2017), https://www.bunkered.co.uk/,
https://www.bunkered.co.uk/golf-news/meet-bob-parsons-war-vet-dot-com-billionaire-pxg-owner.
[67] Monte Burke, "GoDaddy Billionaire Founder Bob Parsons On His Passion For Golf And Motorcycles," Forbes, accessed April 4, 2022, https://www.forbes.com/sites/monteburke/2017/10/18/godaddy-billionaire-founder-bob-parsons-on-his-passion-for-golf-and-motorcycles/.
[68] "StartupJournal | Worthwhile," June 30, 2006,
http://web.archive.org/web/20060630092721/http://www.startupjournal.com/runbusiness/worthwhile/20051207-worthwhile3.html?refresh=on.

time, and particularly when you don't have any people guiding you, you're kind of like a young guy walking into jail for the first time - you learn a lot of lessons. That first year, I priced my software in line with what everybody else was selling theirs for, something like $129. Lost my whole $15,000. The next year, from what I had on a credit card, from my tax loss and from the bonus I got from my day job, I had $25,000. I put all that into the business again and dropped the price to $49. Lost it all again."[69]

On his third try, the business finally took off: a computer magazine in Iowa offered him a lower advertising rate, prompting Parsons to change his marketing techniques once again. The slogan he went with read, 'MoneyCounts - but it only costs twelve bucks.' Besides lowering the price of the software, Parsons also waived its copy protection and licensing requirements, allowing users to buy and redistribute it for just $12.[70] He also aggressively marketed the product to those lower tax-bracket clients using mail offers and magazine ads, securing him a wide user base of customers happy with their affordable, effective software.[71] With these changes in place, MoneyCounts was off to the races. In 1984, the year of his third rebrand, Parsons made $287,000 from the software, reinvesting the money into advertising and marketing before quitting his accounting job and working full time for Parsons Technology. Later on in life, with GoDaddy, Parsons would utilize a similar

---

[69] bunkered.co.uk, "Meet Bob Parsons: War Vet, Dot-Com Billionaire, Golf…," text/html, bunkered.co.uk (bunkered.co.uk, October 7, 2017), https://www.bunkered.co.uk/,
https://www.bunkered.co.uk/golf-news/meet-bob-parsons-war-vet-dot-com-billionaire-pxg-owner.

[70] bunkered.co.uk, "Meet Bob Parsons: War Vet, Dot-Com Billionaire, Golf…," text/html, bunkered.co.uk (bunkered.co.uk, October 7, 2017), https://www.bunkered.co.uk/,
https://www.bunkered.co.uk/golf-news/meet-bob-parsons-war-vet-dot-com-billionaire-pxg-owner.

[71] "DNJournal.Com - Underachiever to Overlord: Go Daddy's Bob Parsons Started Slow Before Building Two Business Empires," accessed March 18, 2022,
https://www.dnjournal.com/columns/cover090504.htm.

strategy of undercutting competitors to reach more users. But for now, he was focused on growing his company.

After roughly a decade of growth, Parsons Technology had expanded to employ 1,000 workers by the mid-nineties, securing Parsons roughly 4% of the of the North American software market.[72] Though his business was booming, Parsons wanted out. He felt that the era of softwares like his was coming to a close, stating, "I saw the writing on the wall ... this industry was shrinking."[73] In 1994, he sold the company to Intuit for $64 million, heading to Arizona to enjoy an early retirement, nice weather, and his passion for golf.[74] There, though, he found that a life of leisure was not for him.

Finding that retirement was just plain boring, Parsons decided to put his money, and himself, back to work. In 1997, Parsons invested some of his own money to break into the growing business of the internet. "All I knew was that I wanted to be involved in it," he recalls of the growing dot-com boom. "I just didn't know exactly what I wanted to do."[75] After throwing ideas at the wall for a bit, Parsons landed on the idea of a service for designing websites. He initially named the company Jomax Technologies, after a local road in Scottsdale, Arizona. Jomax ended up becoming a money sink, with Parsons investing $35 million of his own money to grow the young company, at one

---

[72] "Go Daddy's Bob Parsons Takes His Act to a Bigger Stage - December 1, ...," archive.ph, January 30, 2013, https://archive.ph/SMlCU.

[73] David Andersen and Lameen Witter News Marine Corps, "Former Marine, GoDaddy CEO Talks About His Rise to Success," Military.com, April 10, 2019, https://www.military.com/veteran-jobs/career-advice/military-transition/veteran-ceo-of-go-daddy.html.

[74] AZFoothills.com, "GoDaddy Founder Bob Parsons - Easy Rider," AZFoothills.com, accessed April 5, 2022, https://www.arizonafoothillsmagazine.com/features/features/699-godaddy-founder-bob-parsons-easy-rider.html.

[75] bunkered.co.uk, "Meet Bob Parsons: War Vet, Dot-Com Billionaire, Golf...," text/html, bunkered.co.uk (bunkered.co.uk, October 7, 2017), https://www.bunkered.co.uk/, https://www.bunkered.co.uk/golf-news/meet-bob-parsons-war-vet-dot-com-billionaire-pxg-owner.

point running his accounts down to just $6 million, a fraction of his earnings from the sale of Parsons Technology.[76] Continuing to throw things at the wall, the company eventually landed on a product that would help keep the lights on, a DIY web development tool named WebSite Complete.[77] Parsons recalls a low point in his venture with Jomax: "I got pretty low, and in early 2001 I decided to close the company. I flew to Hawaii to take a little time off and think about how I was going to close it down. But, while I was there, I decided that was not what I wanted to do. The epiphany came when I saw a guy parking cars, and he was really happy. I thought, heck, the worst thing that could happen is I wind up parking pars — or I could go to Vegas and be a stick man at a table — I always thought that was kind of cool. So I came back and said, if the company goes broke, I'll go broke with it."[78]

Even changing the company's name to GoDaddy for marketing purposes didn't produce results, despite the fact that the branding would one day become (in)famous. The name came from a rebranding meeting, Parsons remembers: "We had to change the name. Jomax was so forgettable. We thought and thought and threw out different names. Someone said, 'Big Daddy,' and we checked that. It was gone. I typed in GoDaddy.com, and it was available. I registered it. It is as simple as that. But two things happen when somebody first hears that

---

[76] "Go Daddy's Bob Parsons Takes His Act to a Bigger Stage - December 1, ...," archive.ph, January 30, 2013, https://archive.ph/SMlCU.
[77] "DNJournal.Com - Underachiever to Overlord: Go Daddy's Bob Parsons Started Slow Before Building Two Business Empires," accessed March 18, 2022,
https://www.dnjournal.com/columns/cover090504.htm.
[78] "GoDaddy's Bob Parsons: We're Only Seeing The Tip Of The Iceberg," *Practical Ecommerce* (blog), October 5, 2005,
https://www.practicalecommerce.com/GoDaddy-s-Bob-Parsons-We-re-Only-Seeing-The-Tip-Of-The-Iceberg.

name. They smile, and they remember. So, the name means nothing, it's just there, and it works for us"[79]

The breakthrough came when he pivoted the business towards domain registration. At the time, the domain registration industry was largely controlled by one company, Network Solutions, which charged upwards of $35 per year per domain name.[80] Parsons saw opportunity in the industry: "We had looked at this industry and decided it was both overpriced and under-serviced. However, to make our mark in a field that was being run by monopolies, we had to offer a proposition that no one else was offering at the time."[81] Taking a page from his Parsons Technology days, he settled on acting as the value option in the industry: "We needed something that would make us distinct from the domain name registrars that were already on the market. Therefore, our 'business plan' became low-cost, high-quality products with 24/7 live customer support - that was something the other domain registrars could not compete against. We priced our offering at $8.95 - considerably lower than the hundreds of dollars people originally had paid when the Internet was new, and more than 70 percent lower than the prices they were paying in 1999 when we became a domain registrar. Low prices combined with 24/7 customer support - we could not be touched."[82]

Besides the emphasis on value, competitors in the market also gave props to GoDaddy's range of additional services

---

[79] "GoDaddy's Bob Parsons: We're Only Seeing The Tip Of The Iceberg," *Practical Ecommerce* (blog), October 5, 2005, https://www.practicalecommerce.com/GoDaddy-s-Bob-Parsons-We-re-Only-Seeing-The-Tip-Of-The-Iceberg.
[80] "Go Daddy's Bob Parsons Takes His Act to a Bigger Stage - December 1, ...," archive.ph, January 30, 2013, https://archive.ph/SMlCU.
[81] "DNJournal.Com - Underachiever to Overlord: Go Daddy's Bob Parsons Started Slow Before Building Two Business Empires," accessed March 18, 2022, https://www.dnjournal.com/columns/cover090504.htm.
[82] "DNJournal.Com - Underachiever to Overlord: Go Daddy's Bob Parsons Started Slow Before Building Two Business Empires," accessed March 18, 2022, https://www.dnjournal.com/columns/cover090504.htm.

offered (such as server hosting and e-commerce support): "Attributing their success only to price really sells them short," stated a competitor in an interview. "Bob took advantage of the fact that the largest players didn't offer high-quality service or features."[83] There was also an advantage to offering these services to customers: at the time of GoDaddy's founding, .com domain names were all held by VeriSign, which charged $6 a pop. Offering services like e-commerce support, server hosting, and anonymizing domain registrations allowed GoDaddy to diversify their revenue streams and expand their margins.

Despite the lower price point proving to be effective, the business still stayed grounded until a total stroke of luck, at least for Parsons: the dot-com bubble burst. While other businesses were no longer solvent, GoDaddy kept its cash flow due to its wide user base. Using this cash, Parsons was able to buy out ads which were originally outside his price point. Parsons recalled the moment his company turned a profit while others crumbled, saying, "Everybody we were competing with for advertising all disappeared. Dot-com company after dot-com company folded. We'd be doing business with somebody and - BAM! - they weren't there anymore. So, when it came to buying advertising, I had people standing in line to give it to me. I suddenly had more friends than I thought. We turned the corner that October and, since then, the company hasn't missed a month of being profitable."[84] His focus on memorable marketing under the GoDaddy name had just begun. From there on out, the company grew its brand under its impactful marketing.

Another stroke of luck helped the GoDaddy marketing department in 2005. The company had spent $10 million for a pair of ads parodying Janet Jackson's infamous halftime

---

[83] "Who's Your Go Daddy? - Dec. 18, 2006," accessed March 18, 2022, https://money.cnn.com/2006/12/18/magazines/business2/godaddy.biz2/index.htm.

[84] bunkered.co.uk, "Meet Bob Parsons: War Vet, Dot-Com Billionaire, Golf...," text/html, bunkered.co.uk (bunkered.co.uk, October 7, 2017), https://www.bunkered.co.uk/, https://www.bunkered.co.uk/golf-news/meet-bob-parsons-war-vet-dot-com-billionaire-pxg-owner.

wardrobe malfunction to run during the Super Bowl. After the first one ran, however, the NFL nixed the second ad. While his team were pissed at losing half of their investment, Parsons looked at the rug-pull differently: "I turned to my chief operating guy and said, 'Can we be this lucky to have this happen?'" he recalls.[85] Using the canceled ad as free press, GoDaddy hosted the video elsewhere, labeling it as "Too Hot For The Super Bowl." The GoDaddy name caught fire following the stunt, and the company's market share jumped from 16% to 25% overnight. Parsons and GoDaddy were ready for the sudden expansion, somehow, and their expanded market share held strong. The next year, GoDaddy's market share rose to 34%, then to 46% the year after, even growing through the 2008 recession and reaching 70% in 2017,.[86] The company was able to convert on its 1 minute and 48 seconds of Super Bowl ad fame, growing to unexpected heights thanks to its marketing and a stroke of luck.

While GoDaddy has since toned down its marketing strategy (though the controversial ads ran during Super Bowls for a decade after the initial GoDaddy scandal), it remains a force to be reckoned with almost 25 years after the founding of Jomax Technologies. In 2021, the company served 20 million customers, earned over $3 billion in revenue, and employed over 9,000 people. The company announced its IPO in June of 2014, at the same time that Parsons announced his amicable departure

---

[85] bunkered.co.uk, "Meet Bob Parsons: War Vet, Dot-Com Billionaire, Golf...," text/html, bunkered.co.uk (bunkered.co.uk, October 7, 2017), https://www.bunkered.co.uk/,
https://www.bunkered.co.uk/golf-news/meet-bob-parsons-war-vet-dot-com-billionaire-pxg-owner.

[86] bunkered.co.uk, "Meet Bob Parsons: War Vet, Dot-Com Billionaire, Golf...," text/html, bunkered.co.uk (bunkered.co.uk, October 7, 2017), https://www.bunkered.co.uk/,
https://www.bunkered.co.uk/golf-news/meet-bob-parsons-war-vet-dot-com-billionaire-pxg-owner.

from the company. He sold 72% of his stake in GoDaddy for $2.25 billion to focus on other ventures[87].

Now, Parsons is happily retired – or as retired as he can be. After selling GoDaddy, he put more of his time into YAM Worldwide, Inc. (the YAM stands for "You're a Mess"), his passion project which he founded in 2012.[88] The company operates in a variety of fields, from golf club production to real estate to moviemaking.[89] He also works with The Bob & Renee Parsons Foundation, which he founded with his wife Renee (who runs the day-to-day of the foundation) in 2012, which provides support to a variety of causes, including disaster response and veterans' care.[90]

In recent years, Parsons has opened up more about his experiences with PTSD after his tour in Vietnam. He's lost a friend he served with to mental health concerns and drug addiction, and has also spoken to the press about his mental health issues. Instead of drugs, he says, he was addicted to work: "Everything that I did was solitary. I played tennis, but only singles. I played golf, which you can do by yourself. I got into computer programming — I mean I can't think of a more solitary thing than that. It was the one place where I was OK."[91] He felt

---

[87] Monte Burke, "GoDaddy Billionaire Founder Bob Parsons On His Passion For Golf And Motorcycles," Forbes, accessed April 4, 2022, https://www.forbes.com/sites/monteburke/2017/10/18/godaddy-billionaire-founder-bob-parsons-on-his-passion-for-golf-and-motorcycles/.
[88] "Bob Parsons Rebrands Scottsdale PR Firm Martz Parsons as Big YAM," Phoenix Business Journal, accessed April 6, 2022, https://www.bizjournals.com/phoenix/blog/business/2015/06/why-bob-parsons-changed-the-name-of-his-pr-company.html.
[89] "YAM Worldwide Jobs: Overview | YAM Worldwide," accessed April 5, 2022, https://careers.yamww.com/.
[90] Julie Bort, "Why GoDaddy's Founder Bob Parsons Is Leaving The Company," Business Insider, accessed April 6, 2022, https://www.businessinsider.com/godaddys-founder-bob-parsons-exits-2014-6.
[91] Dan O'Neill, "The Marines 'Totally' Turned Around Bob Parsons and He Won't Stop Paying That Forward," Morning Read, accessed April 6, 2022, https://www.si.com/golf/news/the-marines-turned-around-bob-parsons-and-hell-never-stop-paying-that-forward.

unable to connect to the people around him and instead chose to build himself with the discipline instilled in him by his time as a Marine. After years of different treatments, though, Parsons has worked himself out of that hole and credits his time in the service with giving him the perspective and discipline he needed to succeed.

IV.

Ross Perot

U.S. Navy

Electronic Data Systems

Ross Perot was born Henry Ray Perot on June 27, 1930 in Texarkana, Texas, a town located on the border of Texas and Arkansas.[92] He was the third child of Gabriel Ross Perot, a commodity broker specializing in cotton contracts and part-time horse trader, and Lulu May Ray, a secretary.[93] From a young age, Perot was a dedicated child. He started his working life at just 8 years old as a paperboy for the Texarkana Gazette while also being trained by his father to make a profit by buying and selling bridles to help with the elder Perot's side business.[94,95] Keeping this pattern, Perot would hold odd jobs the rest of his teenage years while attending Texarkana schools for both high school and college.[96] The town, split down the middle by the Texas-Arkansas state border, was a distinctly interesting place: on the Texas side, the town was dry and home to an abundance of churches, but in Arkansas, liquor stores ruled the streets.[97] Here, Perot grew up traditional, Southern, and Christian: he joined the Boy Scouts (becoming an Eagle Scout within 1 year, an achievement which takes 4-6 years on average), attended mass every Sunday, and

---

[92] "Ross Perot, Self-Made Billionaire, Patriot and Philanthropist, Dies at 89," Dallas News, July 9, 2019, https://www.dallasnews.com/business/2019/07/09/ross-perot-self-made-billionaire-patriot-and-philanthropist-dies-at-89/.

[93] Harold Jackson, "Ross Perot Obituary," *The Guardian*, July 9, 2019, sec. US news, https://www.theguardian.com/us-news/2019/jul/09/ross-perot-obituary.

[94] "Ross Perot, Self-Made Billionaire, Patriot and Philanthropist, Dies at 89," Dallas News, July 9, 2019, https://www.dallasnews.com/business/2019/07/09/ross-perot-self-made-billionaire-patriot-and-philanthropist-dies-at-89/.

[95] Kate Sullivan Vries Marlena Baldacci,Karl de, "Ross Perot, Billionaire Tycoon and 2-Time Presidential Candidate, Dies at 89 | CNN Politics," CNN, July 9, 2019, https://www.cnn.com/2019/07/09/politics/ross-perot-dead/index.html.

[96] Harold Jackson, "Ross Perot Obituary," *The Guardian*, July 9, 2019, sec. US news, https://www.theguardian.com/us-news/2019/jul/09/ross-perot-obituary.

[97] Newsweek Staff, "Deep In The Heart Of Texarkana," Newsweek, June 28, 1992, https://www.newsweek.com/deep-heart-texarkana-199530.

learned topics like table manners and ballroom dancing at his alma mater, Patty Hill School.[98,99,100]

After graduating from Texarkana Junior College in 1949, Perot's father urged him to join the military. Enrolling at the U.S. Naval Academy that same year, Perot quickly rose to the top: by the end of his plebe (first) year, he was elected class president and tested first in his class for military aptitude.[101] By his first class (senior) year, Perot had played intramural soccer, coxswained a rowing crew, and served as First Battalion Commander, the third highest rank for a midshipman. According to the Naval Academy itself, Perot also put his Eagle Scout service to use at the school, becoming "an integral part of developing the Naval Academy's Honor Concept, which remains crucial to the Naval Academy's mission to this day."[102] One classmate even wrote in his yearbook, "As president of the Class of '53 he listened to all gripes, then went ahead and did something about them. To say that Ross will be a valuable addition to any branch of the service is an understatement."[103] Topping off his Naval Academy experience, Perot also met his

---

[98] Michael Freeman, "Ross Perot, Longtime Supporter of Scouting, Passes Away at Age 89," Bryan on Scouting, July 10, 2019, https://blog.scoutingmagazine.org/2019/07/10/ross-perot-longtime-supporter-of-scouting-passes-away-at-age-89/.

[99] Newsweek Staff, "Deep In The Heart Of Texarkana," Newsweek, June 28, 1992, https://www.newsweek.com/deep-heart-texarkana-199530.

[100] Cole, "How Long It Takes To Become An Eagle Scout & What To Know," *ScoutSmarts* (blog), December 16, 2019, https://scoutsmarts.com/timeline-and-info-for-becoming-an-eagle-scout/.

[101] "USNA MOURNS PASSING OF DISTINGUISHED GRADUATE H. ROSS PEROT," accessed April 12, 2022, https://www.usna.edu/NewsCenter/2019/07/USNA_MOURNS_PASSING_OF_DISTINGUISHED_GRADUATE_H._ROSS_PEROT.php.

[102] "USNA MOURNS PASSING OF DISTINGUISHED GRADUATE H. ROSS PEROT," accessed April 12, 2022, https://www.usna.edu/NewsCenter/2019/07/USNA_MOURNS_PASSING_OF_DISTINGUISHED_GRADUATE_H._ROSS_PEROT.php.

[103] "USNA MOURNS PASSING OF DISTINGUISHED GRADUATE H. ROSS PEROT," accessed April 12, 2022, https://www.usna.edu/NewsCenter/2019/07/USNA_MOURNS_PASSING_OF_DISTINGUISHED_GRADUATE_H._ROSS_PEROT.php.

wife-to-be, Margot Birmingham, on a blind date during his time at the school.[104] Despite his excellence at the Academy, Perot secretly chafed under the rigid structures of the military, writing home to his parents often to complain about his schooling.[105]

After graduating from the Naval Academy, Perot went into service for four years, first on the destroyer USS Sigourney, and later on the aircraft carrier USS Leyte.[106] During this time, Perot saw no combat but reached the rank of Lieutenant, still annoyed by the military hierarchy, especially the wait in line to be promoted.[107] Finishing his commission in 1957, Perot was finally able to return home, but continued his service as a member of the Naval reserve until 1961. While he saw no combat during his service, Perot learned a lot about himself during his time with the Navy, and would soon put his ambitions to practice.

Before breaking free from the chains of bureaucracies, though, Perot would give working under a large organization one last chance. Taking a job at IBM, Perot's excellence once again shone through: he quickly became a top computer salesman at the company, to the extent that IBM considered cutting back his sales territory to prevent him making too much in commissions.[108] To keep his territory intact, Perot told his superiors that he would cut back his commission rate instead

---

[104] "Ross Perot, Self-Made Billionaire, Patriot and Philanthropist, Dies at 89," Dallas News, July 9, 2019,
https://www.dallasnews.com/business/2019/07/09/ross-perot-self-made-billionaire-patriot-and-philanthropist-dies-at-89/.
[105] Harold Jackson, "Ross Perot Obituary," *The Guardian*, July 9, 2019, sec. US news,
https://www.theguardian.com/us-news/2019/jul/09/ross-perot-obituary.
[106] "Veteran Tributes," accessed April 15, 2022,
http://veterantributes.org/TributeDetail.php?recordID=103.
[107] Robert D. McFadden, "Ross Perot, Brash Texas Billionaire Who Ran for President, Dies at 89," *The New York Times*, July 9, 2019, sec. U.S.,
https://www.nytimes.com/2019/07/09/us/politics/ross-perot-death.html.
[108] "Entrepreneur Extraordinaire | Ross Perot," accessed April 15, 2022,
https://www.rossperot.com/life-story/entrepreneur-extraordinaire.

(IBM eventually decided to cap commissions to salesmen across the company).[109] In 1962, his fifth year, Perot filled his commission cap within the first three weeks of January.[110] Finding himself too big for his small pond once again, Perot tried to think outside the box. One thing he'd noticed from talking to his clients was that they wanted more than just the machines: "What I gleaned from my customers was that they were desperate for more than the hardware. They wanted a finished product. They wanted the hardware, the software, the programming and operations, all optimized for their particular businesses, all at a predetermined price," he recalls.[111] He pitched the idea of selling hardware/software packages to the higher-ups at IBM, but his idea was shot down as the company felt no need to expand its market due to its monopoly on the hardware market. Perot left the company after his pitch failed in order to build bigger and better things on his own.

After leaving IBM, despite his success within the company, Perot had little to his name. He wanted to build a company based on the idea that he pitched at IBM, focused on providing software services to businesses who wanted to use their expensive computers to their fullest potential. To do so, he needed capital. Lacking the funds, he turned to his wife, Margot, who he'd married in 1957. She saw the vision her husband had for the business and fully believed in both its success and Perot's ability to push the idea to its full potential. She lent her husband $1,000 from the money she'd made teaching, money which Perot used to incorporate Electronic Data Services (EDS) on June 27, 1962 – his 32nd birthday.[112]

---

[109] "Entrepreneur Extraordinaire | Ross Perot," accessed April 15, 2022, https://www.rossperot.com/life-story/entrepreneur-extraordinaire.
[110] Robert D. McFadden, "Ross Perot, Brash Texas Billionaire Who Ran for President, Dies at 89," *The New York Times*, July 9, 2019, sec. U.S., https://www.nytimes.com/2019/07/09/us/politics/ross-perot-death.html.
[111] "Entrepreneur Extraordinaire | Ross Perot," accessed April 15, 2022, https://www.rossperot.com/life-story/entrepreneur-extraordinaire.
[112] "Entrepreneur Extraordinaire | Ross Perot," accessed April 15, 2022, https://www.rossperot.com/life-story/entrepreneur-extraordinaire.

The concept for EDS grew from the idea he pitched to his managers at IBM. Perot saw that corporations who were shifting to new computer systems from old-fashioned paper pushing were not using their systems efficiently. His company promised to help crunch data in large numbers using computers. He summed up EDS' services as, "We help companies make maximum use of their new computing power. And do whatever it takes to do that. If I have to move a cot into the data processing room and stay overnight, I do it."[113] He purchased time on an IBM 7070 at Southwestern Life Insurance in Dallas during the company's off hours to give EDS the capacity to process data.[114] To do any computing, though, EDS first needed customers. Perot traveled the country reaching out to prospective clients, making contact 77 times with in-person or telephone sales calls before landing the company its first job.[115] The client, Collins Radio, was a communications company located in Iowa which supplied airlines and the Air Force with radar and radio equipment.[116] The company needed help processing a backlog of order data, and EDS' services were just what they needed. To help with the workload, Perot hired two computer experts on a part-time basis to help him with the project after they got off work. Together, the three of them finished the Collins Radio job in just six weeks, securing EDS enough funding to hire permanent employees for the first time.[117] The company continued to grow through the end

---

[113] "On Its 60th Anniversary, Ross Perot's Electronic Data Systems Stirs Loyalty and Strong Memories," Dallas News, February 10, 2022, https://www.dallasnews.com/opinion/commentary/2022/02/10/on-its-60th-anniversary-ross-perots-electronic-data-systems-stirs-loyalty-and-strong-memories/.
[114] "History of Electronic Data Systems Corporation – FundingUniverse," accessed April 19, 2022, http://www.fundinguniverse.com/company-histories/electronic-data-systems-corporation-history/.
[115] "Entrepreneur Extraordinaire | Ross Perot," accessed April 18, 2022, https://www.rossperot.com/life-story/entrepreneur-extraordinaire.
[116] "Rockwell Collins History," accessed April 19, 2022, https://www.rockwellcollins.com/landing/history-timeline.aspx.
[117] "Entrepreneur Extraordinaire | Ross Perot," accessed April 18, 2022, https://www.rossperot.com/life-story/entrepreneur-extraordinaire.

of 1962, expanding to include a staff of engineers and salespeople. By 1963, Perot snagged his first long-term contract, this time with Frito-Lay, to process their data.[118]

Perot was building his business in a newly budding industry. As such, he made up many practices as he went. To legitimize his business, he charged Frito-Lay strange amounts as monthly costs: "I billed Frito-Lay $5,128 a month for data processing," he recalled. "I used odd numbers like 5,128 in those days to make it look like I knew exactly what I was doing and had figured everything down to the last penny."[119] He also established billing practices in order to secure EDS more money up front: "I tell my clients, 'You have to pay in advance.' And when they ask why, I say, 'It's customary in the computer services industry.' But the business is so new, there are no customs yet. I'm making them up as I go along.'"[120]

Besides establishing his own external processes, Perot also organized EDS to his own liking. First, he focused on hiring self-motivated, ambitious people: his first hire, Tom Marquez, recalls: "We used to say the kind of guy we wouldn't want around EDS was a lazy genius. Ross is very, very interested in people living up to their potential."[121] For this reason, he often hired ex-military personnel, as he found they were more likely to be

---

[118] "On Its 60th Anniversary, Ross Perot's Electronic Data Systems Stirs Loyalty and Strong Memories," Dallas News, February 10, 2022, https://www.dallasnews.com/opinion/commentary/2022/02/10/on-its-60th-anniversary-ross-perots-electronic-data-systems-stirs-loyalty-and-strong-memories/.

[119] "On Its 60th Anniversary, Ross Perot's Electronic Data Systems Stirs Loyalty and Strong Memories," Dallas News, February 10, 2022, https://www.dallasnews.com/opinion/commentary/2022/02/10/on-its-60th-anniversary-ross-perots-electronic-data-systems-stirs-loyalty-and-strong-memories/.

[120] "On Its 60th Anniversary, Ross Perot's Electronic Data Systems Stirs Loyalty and Strong Memories," Dallas News, February 10, 2022, https://www.dallasnews.com/opinion/commentary/2022/02/10/on-its-60th-anniversary-ross-perots-electronic-data-systems-stirs-loyalty-and-strong-memories/.

[121] "A Tough Boss at EDS, Perot Now a Competitor," AP NEWS, accessed April 19, 2022, https://apnews.com/article/b6129d57f397434716957e81cfcbb770.

self-motivated and accepting of his leadership. Perot ran a very tight ship, enforcing dress codes described as "conservative" and "military-style", demanding 24-hour availability, and at one point only hiring married men (he felt bachelors might leave the company too quickly).[122,123] Employees that put up with his harsh leadership were rewarded handsomely: many employees made pretty sums due to the company's stock options, Perot would often take time to help employees' families in need, and benefits were equal across the board – "The guy cutting the grass at my house has the same health plan I have," Perot once stated.[124]

In 1979, the American public learned just how far Perot would go for his employees: a pair of his top employees were being held hostage by Iranian authorities as the Iranian Revolution raged around them. The men were in the country as part of a contract to install modern computing and healthcare systems for the former Shah Mohammed Reza Pahlavi, but unfortunately for them the situation turned sour when the Shah was ousted and replaced with Ayatollah Sayyid Ruhollah Khomeini.[125] Most of the other 130 EDS employees had been evacuated for safety reasons as soon as the revolution began, but a skeleton crew remained to wrap up operations before leaving. As the head of his company, Perot pledged to bring the two men home safely. The diplomatic approach failed to see the two employees free, so Perot took matters into his own hands, creating a plan and forming a team of six ex-military EDS employees to get their fellow workers home safely. In a plan which involved the EDS men inciting a riot, storming the Iranian

---

[122] "A Tough Boss at EDS, Perot Now a Competitor," AP NEWS, accessed April 19, 2022,
https://apnews.com/article/b6129d57f397434716957e81cfcbb770.
[123] "History of Electronic Data Systems Corporation – FundingUniverse," accessed April 19, 2022,
http://www.fundinguniverse.com/company-histories/electronic-data-systems-corporation-history/.
[124] "A Tough Boss at EDS, Perot Now a Competitor," AP NEWS, accessed April 19, 2022,
https://apnews.com/article/b6129d57f397434716957e81cfcbb770.
[125] "Iran Hostage Rescue | Ross Perot," accessed April 21, 2022,
https://www.rossperot.com/life-story/iran-hostage-rescue.

prison, and freeing the two employees and thousands of other employees, the company recovered its most valuable assets safely, and with much media attention. "We tried the government. No luck. We tried to work through the Iranian legal system. We even tried to pay bail, which was nothing more than a ransom," Perot recalled. "Everything failed. I was either going to lose the guys or try something...We took the risk because we felt it was wrong to leave two innocent men behind. It was that simple. It was the principle."[126]

After establishing EDS' sustainability with the long-term Frito-Lay contract, Perot was able to keep the business chugging along, growing slowly over the years with other new contracts. But the company's really big break came in 1965, when President Lyndon B. Johnson signed Medicare into law with H.R. 6675.[127] This new government program, set up to provide healthcare to millions of Americans, required vast amounts of paperwork, in such great amounts that computers were needed to adequately keep the system moving. As the program was established and expanded throughout the 1970s, EDS snatched up Medicare data processing contracts state by state, developing software specifically dedicated to handling the new program's data.[128] Copyrighting the software, EDS forced the federal government to

---

[126] "Iran Hostage Rescue | Ross Perot," accessed April 21, 2022, https://www.rossperot.com/life-story/iran-hostage-rescue.
[127] "H.R.6675 - 89th Congress (1965-1966): An Act to Provide a Hospital Insurance Program for the Aged under the Social Security Act with a Supplementary Health Benefits Program and an Expanded Program of Medical Assistance, to Increase Benefits under the Old-Age, Survivors, and Disability Insurance System, to Improve the Federal-State Public Assistance Programs, and for Other Purposes," legislation, July 30, 1965, 1965/1966,
https://www.congress.gov/bill/89th-congress/house-bill/6675.
[128] Harold Jackson, "Ross Perot Obituary," *The Guardian*, July 9, 2019, sec. US news,
https://www.theguardian.com/us-news/2019/jul/09/ross-perot-obituary.

pay royalties for its use, growing the company's profits to 30% a year and setting it up for real financial success.[129]

In 1968, Perot made EDS public, personally owning 10 million shares of the company.[130] On the day of the IPO, EDS stock was worth $23 per share, earning Perot a cool $230 million.[131] The stock's value would eventually reach $162, making Perot a billionaire and many of his employees millionaires thanks to the company's generous stock options.[132] Post-IPO, the company continued to flourish, blazing a trail for other companies to follow in the now-ubiquitous technology services space. In a time when personal computers seemed like an impossibility, computing was seen as expensive and specific to certain large corporations.[133] Pushing this perception aside, Perot secured deals with companies in an ever-increasing number of industries, from insurance to banking to travel booking, contributing in part to the acceptance of computers as efficient tools for modern society.[134] Other companies would eventually

---

[129] Harold Jackson, "Ross Perot Obituary," *The Guardian*, July 9, 2019, sec. US news, https://www.theguardian.com/us-news/2019/jul/09/ross-perot-obituary.

[130] "On Its 60th Anniversary, Ross Perot's Electronic Data Systems Stirs Loyalty and Strong Memories," Dallas News, February 10, 2022, https://www.dallasnews.com/opinion/commentary/2022/02/10/on-its-60th-anniversary-ross-perots-electronic-data-systems-stirs-loyalty-and-strong-memories/.

[131] "On Its 60th Anniversary, Ross Perot's Electronic Data Systems Stirs Loyalty and Strong Memories," Dallas News, February 10, 2022, https://www.dallasnews.com/opinion/commentary/2022/02/10/on-its-60th-anniversary-ross-perots-electronic-data-systems-stirs-loyalty-and-strong-memories/.

[132] Robert D. McFadden, "Ross Perot, Brash Texas Billionaire Who Ran for President, Dies at 89," *The New York Times*, July 9, 2019, sec. U.S., https://www.nytimes.com/2019/07/09/us/politics/ross-perot-death.html.

[133] "Ross Perot Sr. Used His Time at IBM and $1,000 to Help Change an Industry – and DFW," Dallas Business Journal, accessed April 21, 2022, https://www.bizjournals.com/dallas/news/2019/07/10/ross-perot-sr.html.

[134] "Entrepreneur Extraordinaire | Ross Perot," accessed April 18, 2022, https://www.rossperot.com/life-story/entrepreneur-extraordinaire.

develop their own computing systems, eliminating the need for EDS to process their data externally, but Perot would expand EDS' operations to help others install and coordinate their systems, while also keeping up lucrative government contracts. While the company's stock price would fluctuate greatly over the next decade (with Perot losing roughly $500 million in just one day), the company steadily grew over the years, doubling from 1964 to 1970 before slowing to 22 percent in 1971 and 13 percent by 1977.[135,136]

In 1984, Perot decided to sell EDS to General Motors for $2.6 billion.[137] GM was looking to fix its data processing system, which was costing the company $6 billion annually before the purchase.[138] As part of the sale, Perot held on to just enough EDS shares to snag a place on GM's board. At GM, Perot's issues with authority and bureaucracy flared up again: "Revitalizing GM is like teaching an elephant to tap dance," he recalled. "It takes five years to design a new car in this country. Heck, we won World War II in four years."[139] Besides the company not moving as quickly as Perot would like, he also clashed with GM chairman Roger Smith over how he treated his employees, pointing out

---

[135] "Ross Perot, Billionaire Who Sought Presidency, Dies at 89," *Bloomberg.Com*, July 9, 2019, https://www.bloomberg.com/news/articles/2019-07-09/h-ross-perot-billionaire-who-sought-presidency-dies-at-89.

[136] "History of Electronic Data Systems Corporation – FundingUniverse," accessed April 19, 2022, http://www.fundinguniverse.com/company-histories/electronic-data-systems-corporation-history/.

[137] "Ross Perot, Self-Made Billionaire, Patriot and Philanthropist, Dies at 89," Dallas News, July 9, 2019, https://www.dallasnews.com/business/2019/07/09/ross-perot-self-made-billionaire-patriot-and-philanthropist-dies-at-89/.

[138] "History of Electronic Data Systems Corporation – FundingUniverse," accessed April 19, 2022, http://www.fundinguniverse.com/company-histories/electronic-data-systems-corporation-history/.

[139] Robert D. McFadden, "Ross Perot, Brash Texas Billionaire Who Ran for President, Dies at 89," *The New York Times*, July 9, 2019, sec. U.S., https://www.nytimes.com/2019/07/09/us/politics/ross-perot-death.html.

that two of the company's lower-level pension plans were underfunded while executive plans were functioning perfectly.[140] The toxic relationship even became public news, with Perot saying, "The first EDSer to see a snake kills it. At GM, first thing you do is organize a committee on snakes. Then you bring in a consultant who knows a lot about snakes. Third thing you do is talk about it for a year," in an interview with BusinessWeek.[141] Eventually, Perot left GM, selling his remaining portion of EDS to GM for $700 million. EDS would eventually be sold off by GM for $25 billion in 1996 before landing in the hands of Hewlett-Packard in 2006 for the sum of $13.9 billion, where it was rebranded to HP Enterprise Services.[142]

After leaving GM and all its bureaucratic speed bumps in his rearview mirror, Perot set out to found a new company in the data processing industry. Founded in 1988, his new project Perot Systems grew even more rapidly than EDS had at its onset, becoming 25% larger within seven years than EDS was at the same time in its journey.[143] Using his prior experience and established reputation in the industry, the company soared to great heights: its stock offering opened in 1999, the company became part of the Fortune 1000, and, at its peak, Perot Systems employed over 24,000 employees and owned offices in 25 different countries.[144] Another of Perot's ventures saw him as the

---

[140] "Ross Perot, Self-Made Billionaire, Patriot and Philanthropist, Dies at 89," Dallas News, July 9, 2019, https://www.dallasnews.com/business/2019/07/09/ross-perot-self-made-billionaire-patriot-and-philanthropist-dies-at-89/.
[141] "Ross Perot, Billionaire Who Sought Presidency, Dies at 89," Bloomberg.Com, July 9, 2019, https://www.bloomberg.com/news/articles/2019-07-09/h-ross-perot-billionaire-who-sought-presidency-dies-at-89.
[142] "Ross Perot's Former Companies Helped Shape Washington's Tech Space," Washington Business Journal, accessed April 21, 2022, https://www.bizjournals.com/washington/news/2019/07/09/ross-perot-s-former-companies-helped-shape-greater.html.
[143] "Entrepreneur Extraordinaire | Ross Perot," accessed April 18, 2022, https://www.rossperot.com/life-story/entrepreneur-extraordinaire.
[144] "Entrepreneur Extraordinaire | Ross Perot," accessed April 18, 2022, https://www.rossperot.com/life-story/entrepreneur-extraordinaire.

first angel investor in NeXT, a computer and software company founded by one Steve Jobs after his 1985 split from Apple. Perot provided Jobs with $20 million and insights into leadership which would prove key to the growth of NeXT, which would go on to become core to Apple as we know it today: "The thing that impressed me most about Ross was that, while most people focus on the bottom line – which he certainly did – what Ross looked at first was what I call the 'top-line' – which is the people and the strategy," Jobs recalled of Perot and the lessons he learned from their partnership.[145]

Besides his spectacular business successes, Ross Perot is widely known for one other thing: his independent bid for the presidency. Before the 1992 presidential election, Perot had had some brushes with the U.S. government and the media. In 1969, he attempted to airlift 30 tons of food, medicines, and gifts to a group of American prisoners of war in Vietnam, inspired by their plight and frustrated with the lack of support for them in America.[146] While his supply drop (which was unauthorized by Washington) was turned back in Hanoi, the gesture brought much attention to the suffering of POWs during the Vietnam War while also increasing Perot's frustration with government and bureaucracy.[147] More locally, Perot had a hand in a few pieces of Texas legislation, including a 1979 toughening of state drug sentencing and a 1983 overhaul of the state education

---

[145] "Entrepreneur Extraordinaire | Ross Perot," accessed April 18, 2022, https://www.rossperot.com/life-story/entrepreneur-extraordinaire.

[146] Robert D. McFadden, "Ross Perot, Brash Texas Billionaire Who Ran for President, Dies at 89," *The New York Times*, July 9, 2019, sec. U.S., https://www.nytimes.com/2019/07/09/us/politics/ross-perot-death.html.

[147] Harold Jackson, "Ross Perot Obituary," *The Guardian*, July 9, 2019, sec. US news, https://www.theguardian.com/us-news/2019/jul/09/ross-perot-obituary.

system, which increased education taxes and limited class sizes, among other changes.[148]

In 1992, Perot leveraged the folk legend garnered from his Vietnam and Iran stunts and announced that he would be running for president in the year's election. His campaign began on February 20, 1992, when Perot appeared on CNN's "Larry King Live."[149] When King asked his guest if he would run for president that year, Perot first answered with a clear "no." But by the end of the show, after pumping up his image and discussing the challenges facing America, he stated that he would be willing to make a bid for the presidency if "you, the people, are that serious." First, he stated, he would need his supporters to get his name on the ballot in all 50 states. People dissatisfied with the state of America and the establishment political parties put their weight behind him, getting Perot onto ballots nationwide as an Independent alongside Democrat Bill Clinton and the Republican incumbent George H.W. Bush.[150]

Both Perot's platform and his campaign were scattershot and inconsistent, but the man succeeded in capturing the public's attention like no independent candidate had in almost a century. With a focus on TV and radio ads, Perot put his fortune from EDS and Perot Systems to work, spending over $31.9 million on TV spots alone (Clinton spent $32.7 million on TV, while Bush came in at $27.7 million).[151] Over the airwaves, Perot fired memorable shots at the federal government, calling a hole

---

[148] Robert D. McFadden, "Ross Perot, Brash Texas Billionaire Who Ran for President, Dies at 89," *The New York Times*, July 9, 2019, sec. U.S., https://www.nytimes.com/2019/07/09/us/politics/ross-perot-death.html.

[149] "Ross Perot, Billionaire Who Sought Presidency, Dies at 89," *Bloomberg.Com*, July 9, 2019, https://www.bloomberg.com/news/articles/2019-07-09/h-ross-perot-billionaire-who-sought-presidency-dies-at-89.

[150] "Ross Perot, Billionaire Who Sought Presidency, Dies at 89," *Bloomberg.Com*, July 9, 2019, https://www.bloomberg.com/news/articles/2019-07-09/h-ross-perot-billionaire-who-sought-presidency-dies-at-89.

[151] "The Presidency's Price Tag," USC News, August 27, 1995, https://news.usc.edu/20509/The-presidency-s-price-tag/.

in national accounts "like a crazy aunt you keep down in the basement" and comparing the U.S. tax system to "an old inner tube that's been patched by every special interest in the country."[152] Some of his ads consisted of 30-minute "infomercials" where he outlined his positions, earning him ratings that sometimes outstripped those of the most popular sitcoms of the time, and he made many appearances on talk shows, pushing his image to their dedicated audiences.[153]

Perot ran on a conservative platform with his own twist, advocating cuts in government spending, reductions in the federal deficit, and looser gun control, also pushing for electronic town halls where Americans could give feedback on how representatives should vote on laws with the push of a button, and called for a return to small-town America, a vision where towns looked like his hometown of Texarkana.[154,155] Ironically, his takes on government bloat and overspending were directly opposite his business interests, as EDS and Perot Systems both relied on government contracts for large portions of their business.[156] Despite this conflict of interest looking back, his platform became a juggernaut in 1992, earning support from

---

[152] Harold Jackson, "Ross Perot Obituary," *The Guardian*, July 9, 2019, sec. US news, https://www.theguardian.com/us-news/2019/jul/09/ross-perot-obituary.

[153] Robert D. McFadden, "Ross Perot, Brash Texas Billionaire Who Ran for President, Dies at 89," *The New York Times*, July 9, 2019, sec. U.S., https://www.nytimes.com/2019/07/09/us/politics/ross-perot-death.html.

[154] Robert D. McFadden, "Ross Perot, Brash Texas Billionaire Who Ran for President, Dies at 89," *The New York Times*, July 9, 2019, sec. U.S., https://www.nytimes.com/2019/07/09/us/politics/ross-perot-death.html.

[155] Jane Coaston, "Ross Perot, the Oddball Presidential Candidate Who Won 20 Million Votes in 1992, Has Died," Vox, July 9, 2019, https://www.vox.com/2019/7/9/20687556/ross-perot-dies-obit-1992-reform-party.

[156] Jane Coaston, "Ross Perot, the Oddball Presidential Candidate Who Won 20 Million Votes in 1992, Has Died," Vox, July 9, 2019, https://www.vox.com/2019/7/9/20687556/ross-perot-dies-obit-1992-reform-party.

both sides of the aisle as Bush and Clinton sparred with one another. He participated in all three presidential debates, poking fun at both parties with equal measure: "It's not the Republicans' fault, of course, and it's not the Democrats' fault," he said in one debate. "Somewhere out there there's an extraterrestrial that's doing this to us, I guess."[157] Perot's vision was gaining momentum, especially with middle-class, moderate voters, and by June of 1992, he was actually leading the race according to some polls.[158]

In July of 1992, Perot stunned the nation, suddenly dropping out of the race. He cited poor polling and "the revitalization of the Democratic Party," but eventually got back to the campaign trail in October, just before voting began.[159,160] Just nine days before the election, Perot revealed his reason for dropping out so suddenly on CBS's "60 Minutes": he stated that Republican leaders planned "to have a computer-created false photo of my daughter, Carolyn, that they were going to give the press shortly before her wedding to embarrass her."[161] He offered no proof for this claim. While his extended absence should have completely taken the wind out of his sails, Perot seemed to still have a hold over a strong portion of America. On election day, he took home 19.7 million (19%) of the 104 million popular votes,

---

[157] Robert D. McFadden, "Ross Perot, Brash Texas Billionaire Who Ran for President, Dies at 89," *The New York Times*, July 9, 2019, sec. U.S.
[158] Jane Coaston, "Ross Perot, the Oddball Presidential Candidate Who Won 20 Million Votes in 1992, Has Died," Vox, July 9, 2019, https://www.vox.com/2019/7/9/20687556/ross-perot-dies-obit-1992-reform-party.
[159] Harold Jackson, "Ross Perot Obituary," *The Guardian*, July 9, 2019, sec. US news, https://www.theguardian.com/us-news/2019/jul/09/ross-perot-obituary.
[160] "Ross Perot, Billionaire Who Sought Presidency, Dies at 89," *Bloomberg.Com*, July 9, 2019, https://www.bloomberg.com/news/articles/2019-07-09/h-ross-perot-billionaire-who-sought-presidency-dies-at-89.
[161] "Ross Perot, Billionaire Who Sought Presidency, Dies at 89," *Bloomberg.Com*, July 9, 2019, https://www.bloomberg.com/news/articles/2019-07-09/h-ross-perot-billionaire-who-sought-presidency-dies-at-89.

the highest percentage of the popular vote earned by an independent candidate since Teddy Roosevelt's bid for the presidency with the Bull Moose Party in 1912.[162] The election ended with Clinton in first place, nabbing 43% of the vote. Perot, despite scoring a historic amount of votes for an independent candidate, failed to secure even a single electoral vote.[163]

Perot would run again in 1996 with his newly-formed Reform Party, but failed to outdo himself. He was barred from the presidential debates because a commission decided he was unlikely to be competitive in the election, and because some ugly details about his dealings leaked out. Some of these details include the facts that he had employees take lie detector tests and that he hired private detectives to investigate some conspiracy theories he believed in.[164] He won 8.4% of the popular vote that year, falling to Clinton yet again. 1996 would spell Perot's last year in politics directly, though he would still use his voice, endorsing George W. Bush in 2000 and Mitt Romney in 2012, also launching a national debt-tracking website in 2008.[165,166]

After politics, Perot continued his life as a businessman as Perot Systems continued to grow. In 2008, Forbes named him

---

[162] Katherine Lam, "Ross Perot's Billion-Dollar Journey, from Top Salesman to Business Magnate," Text.Article, FOXBusiness (Fox Business, July 9, 2019),
https://www.foxbusiness.com/business-leaders/ross-perot-billion-dollar-journey-salesman-business-magnate.
[163] Jane Coaston, "Ross Perot, the Oddball Presidential Candidate Who Won 20 Million Votes in 1992, Has Died," Vox, July 9, 2019,
https://www.vox.com/2019/7/9/20687556/ross-perot-dies-obit-1992-reform-party.
[164] Robert D. McFadden, "Ross Perot, Brash Texas Billionaire Who Ran for President, Dies at 89," *The New York Times*, July 9, 2019, sec. U.S., https://www.nytimes.com/2019/07/09/us/politics/ross-perot-death.html.
[165] Robert D. McFadden, "Ross Perot, Brash Texas Billionaire Who Ran for President, Dies at 89," *The New York Times*, July 9, 2019, sec. U.S., https://www.nytimes.com/2019/07/09/us/politics/ross-perot-death.html.
[166] Harold Jackson, "Ross Perot Obituary," *The Guardian*, July 9, 2019, sec. US news,
https://www.theguardian.com/us-news/2019/jul/09/ross-perot-obituary.

America's 97th richest man with a net worth of $5 billion.[167] He gave his money generously to causes he believed in, with special attention to military veterans: in 1991, Perot donated $2.5 million to research strange neurological symptoms suffered by Gulf War veterans, eventually leading to the discovery of Gulf War Illness by Dr. Robert Haley, for whom he helped secure an additional $5 million in defense funding.[168] In 2009, the Department of Veteran Affairs officially honored his contributions to the veteran community, both for his campaign for POWs in Vietnam and his support for Gulf War Illness research.[169] In 2019, Perot died of leukemia. In 2016, when asked about what he wanted to be remembered for, Perot answered, "Aw, I don't worry about that."[170]

---

[167] Robert D. McFadden, "Ross Perot, Brash Texas Billionaire Who Ran for President, Dies at 89," *The New York Times,* July 9, 2019, sec. U.S., https://www.nytimes.com/2019/07/09/us/politics/ross-perot-death.html.

[168] "Toxic Exposures Caused Illness in Gulf War Veterans | SPH," accessed April 21, 2022, https://www.bu.edu/sph/news/articles/2016/toxic-exposures-caused-illness-in-gulf-war-veterans/.

[169] Office of Public and Intergovernmental Affairs, "VA Salutes Ross Perot," News, accessed April 21, 2022, https://www.va.gov/opa/pressrel/pressrelease.cfm?id=1640.

[170] "Ross Perot, Self-Made Billionaire, Patriot and Philanthropist, Dies at 89," Dallas News, July 9, 2019, https://www.dallasnews.com/business/2019/07/09/ross-perot-self-made-billionaire-patriot-and-philanthropist-dies-at-89/.

V.

Phil Knight

U.S. Army

Nike

Phil Knight was born on February 24, 1938 in Portland, Oregon to Bill Knight and his wife, Lota Cloy Knight. Bill was a gruff but respectable father, a lawyer and former member of the Oregon House of Representatives who worked as publisher for the now-defunct Oregon Journal.[171] Growing up, Phil was a small kid, and was unable to play contact sports in high school.[172] Instead, he ran track as a middle-distance runner. "My father liked sports," Knight recalls. "Sports were always respectable."[173] During one of his high school summers, looking to make some cash, he asked his dad for a summer job at his newspaper. Being a strong-willed self-starter, his father refused to give his son a handout, believing that Phil should make his own path in life.[174] Following his father's advice, Phil grabbed a job at his father's rival paper, The Oregonian. There, he worked night shifts tallying up sports scores and commuted the seven miles between work to home by running.

After graduating from Cleveland High School, Knight enrolled at the University of Oregon, snagging a place on one of the best track programs in the country at the time.[175] The track team's coach was the legendary Bill Bowerman, who would eventually become Knight's business partner at Nike. During his time on the team, Phil would become a guinea pig for Bowerman thanks to his middle-of-the pack status as a runner. Bowerman would constantly tinker with running shoes for the team, believing, according to Knight, that "shaving an ounce off a pair

---

[171] "Eugene Register-Guard - Google News Archive Search." Accessed April 29, 2022.
https://news.google.com/newspapers?id=KxBWAAAAIBAJ&sjid=S-IDAAAAIBAJ&dq=william%20knight%20publisher%20dies&pg=6833%2C5044584.
[172] archive.ph. "Must Be the Shoes - Real People Stories : People.Com," September 9, 2012. https://archive.ph/tdnU.
[173] Knight, Phil. *Shoe Dog: A Memoir by the Creator of Nike*. Reprint edition. Scribner, 2016.
[174] archive.ph. "Must Be the Shoes - Real People Stories : People.Com," September 9, 2012. https://archive.ph/tdnU.
[175] "Phil Knight: The Force Behind Nike," June 25, 2010.
https://web.archive.org/web/20100625221415/http://www.stanfordalumni.org/news/magazine/1997/janfeb/articles/knight.html.

of shoes for a guy running a mile could make a big difference."[176] Thus began Knight's intimate relationship with shoes. He remembers, "I was very aware of shoes when I was running track. The American shoes were offshoots of tire companies. Shoes cost $5, and you would come back from a five-mile run with your feet bleeding. Then the German companies came in with $30 shoes, which were more comfortable."[177] In his senior year on the team, one of his teammates even won the Pacific Coast Conference in a Coach Bowermam-made pair of shoes which were an ounce lighter than other shoes on the market.[178] Even before Nike was a thought in his mind, Knight knew that the footwear market was ripe for innovation. Besides running for Oregon, he also participated in school life in other ways, becoming a brother with the Phi Gamma Delta and working as a sports reporter for the Oregon Daily Emerald, the school's student newspaper.

Knight graduated with a business degree (BBA) from the University of Oregon in just three years with the class of 1959.[179] Following this, he enlisted with the U.S. Army, serving for a year at Fort Lewis in Tacoma, Washington and another year at Fort Eustis in Newport News, Virginia.[180] Knight doesn't talk much about his time with the Army, only saying that he "survived a yearlong hitch in the U.S. Army" in his memoir Shoe Dog: A Memoir by the Creator of Nike, and he hasn't discussed it in any of his relatively rare media appearances, preferring to talk shop

---

[176] "Phil Knight: The Force Behind Nike," June 25, 2010. https://web.archive.org/web/20100625221415/http://www.stanfordalumni.org/news/magazine/1997/janfeb/articles/knight.html.
[177] "Phil Knight: The Force Behind Nike," June 25, 2010. https://web.archive.org/web/20100625221415/http://www.stanfordalumni.org/news/magazine/1997/janfeb/articles/knight.html.
[178] Stanford Graduate School of Business. "Phil Knight, MBA '62: Never Give Up." Accessed May 2, 2022. https://www.gsb.stanford.edu/insights/phil-knight-mba-62-never-give.
[179] Hayward Field, "UNIVERSITY OF OREGON," n.d., 60. https://scholarsbank.uoregon.edu/xmlui/bitstream/handle/1794/13368/UOCAT_Jun_1959_Comm.pdf?sequence=1&isAllowed=y
[180] Knight, Phil. Shoe Dog: A Memoir by the Creator of Nike. Reprint edition. Scribner, 2016.

about Nike's business side instead.[181] After his first year of service, Knight moved on to become a member of the Army Reserves for the next 7 years. One thing to note about his service was its timing: Knight was on active duty during the time between the Korean and Vietnam Wars, and describes himself as being "haunted" by the Vietnam War, both for its pointlessness and its effects on his growing business, which began to take shape as America's involvement in Vietnam grew.[182] Underlying his description of the war during his time as a reservist is his fear of having to join the U.S. Army in a war it was mishandling. As he describes it, the U.S. was in a "fight not to win, but to avoid losing. A surefire losing strategy. My fellow soldiers felt the same way. Is it any wonder that, the moment we were dismissed, we marched double-time to the nearest bar?"[183]

Following his stint with the Army, Knight returned to school, enrolling at the Stanford Graduate School of Business. There, he finally found a passion for academia which he'd lacked before (Stanford magazine characterized him as "an indifferent student").[184] He'd always had passion growing up, but much of that passion couldn't be applied in the classroom and was instead let out on the track: "At different times I'd fantasized about becoming a great novelist, a great journalist, a great statesman. But the ultimate dream was to be a great athlete."[185] Luckily, his passions were allowed to coalesce in one specific class at Stanford: Frank Shallenberger's small-business class, where he wrote a paper titled "Can Japanese Sports Shoes Do to German Sports Shoes What Japanese Cameras Did to German Cameras?"

---

[181] Knight, Phil. *Shoe Dog: A Memoir by the Creator of Nike*. Reprint edition. Scribner, 2016.
[182] Knight, Phil. *Shoe Dog: A Memoir by the Creator of Nike*. Reprint edition. Scribner, 2016.
[183] Knight, Phil. *Shoe Dog: A Memoir by the Creator of Nike*. Reprint edition. Scribner, 2016.
[184] "Phil Knight: The Force Behind Nike," June 25, 2010. https://web.archive.org/web/20100625221415/http://www.stanfordalumni.org/news/magazine/1997/janfeb/articles/knight.html.
[185] Knight, Phil. *Shoe Dog: A Memoir by the Creator of Nike*. Reprint edition. Scribner, 2016.

In the paper, he focused on the problems he'd noticed with German shoes produced by leading brands like Puma and Adidas, and how manufacturing higher-quality shoes in Japan for cheap could revolutionize the shoe business. The paper became a sort of amalgamation of his passions for business, running, and travel. "Being a runner, I knew something about running shoes. Being a business buff, I knew that Japanese cameras had made deep cuts into the camera market, which had once been dominated by the Germans. Thus, I argued that Japanese running shoes might do the same thing," he remembers. "The idea interested me, then inspired me, then captivated me. It seemed so obvious, so simple, so potentially huge."[186] The paper received an A, and Knight spent the rest of his time at Stanford thinking about his "Crazy Idea" and going to Japan to pitch the idea to shoe companies.

Following this impulse, Knight decided to head to Japan after graduating from Stanford in 1962. Before embarking on his part-spiritual journey (Knight buys into many different belief systems from around the world, especially East Asia), part-business trip, he asked his father for both his blessing and money. Bracing himself for rejection, Knight was surprised when his father gave him his begrudging support. Knight had grown up during World War Two listening to reports about the war in the Pacific and fearing Japanese bombers in the sky, so going to Japan may have felt like a dangerous proposition to others in his family, but luckily for him, his father didn't mind.

With money from his father, his part-time jobs, and the sale of his car lining his pocket, Knight headed to Japan by way of Hawaii accompanied by a close friend. In Hawaii he took up surfing and spent time at a handful of sales jobs before heading to Japan alone. Arriving in a partially bombed-out Tokyo still recovering from the war, Knight spent his days visiting local landmarks, from the Tokyo Stock Exchange and fish markets (which stressed him out) to old shrines and temples (which also

---

[186] Knight, Phil. *Shoe Dog: A Memoir by the Creator of Nike*. Reprint edition. Scribner, 2016.

stressed him out but left him more fulfilled).[187] The one industrial feature of Japan that didn't stress him out was the Onitsuka Tiger factory. Onitsuka was a small shoe brand producing running shoes out of Kobe, in southern Japan. Knight had scheduled a meeting with Onitsuka representatives, preceded by a tour of their factory. Inside, he described the factory as "interesting" and "musical," a "cobbler's concerto."[188] Following the tour, he pitched his "Crazy Idea" to the Onitsuka executives, rehashing his presentation for his Stanford paper. When asked the name of the non-existent company he represented, Knight had to think fast, coming up with "Blue Ribbon Sports" on the spot. The executives at Onitsuka were enthusiastic about Knight's pitch. Knight's plan to undercut Adidas and his (dubious, yet prescient) promise of a $1 billion dollar untapped American shoe market made Onitsuka so excited that they began pitching shoes to him. He ended up purchasing samples of a trainer shoe named "Limber Up" for $50, wired to him by his father.[189] After the successful pitch, Knight traveled through Asia, visiting Bombay, Hong Kong, the Philippines, and a Vietnam on the precipice of war before heading to Europe. His almost six-month trip was a success, granting Knight a starting point for his "Crazy Idea" as well as all the worldly adventures a young man could want.

When he returned to Oregon, Knight's first question to his father was, "Did my shoes come?"[190] While he wanted badly for his new business to take off, reality struck, and Knight needed cash. He went back to Portland State to earn his CPA before taking an accounting job at Lybrand, Ross Bros., and Montgomery, a Big Eight accounting firm. Knight worked

---

[187] Knight, Phil. *Shoe Dog: A Memoir by the Creator of Nike*. Reprint edition. Scribner, 2016.
[188] Knight, Phil. *Shoe Dog: A Memoir by the Creator of Nike*. Reprint edition. Scribner, 2016.
[189] Knight, Phil. *Shoe Dog: A Memoir by the Creator of Nike*. Reprint edition. Scribner, 2016.
[190] Knight, Phil. *Shoe Dog: A Memoir by the Creator of Nike*. Reprint edition. Scribner, 2016.

through the drudgery of a normal desk job, waiting until the day his samples came from Onitsuka .

They arrived around Christmas of 1964. He grabbed the samples from the warehouse the first week of the new year, admiring their construction, and sent a pair off to his shoe-obsessed track coach from University of Oregon, Bill Bowerman. Bowerman immediately asked to meet with Knight after he got his hands on the trainers. While Knight had initially wanted to just provide shoes for Oregon's team, Bowerman quickly requested to get in on his idea of reselling the shoes to a larger audience, with each putting up half the cost to order a $1,000 round of shoes from Japan.[191] After talks with a lawyer, Bowerman and Knight solidified the deal, with Knight holding a 51-49 controlling stake in the company. Following signing on with his new business partner, Knight called Onitsuka, asking that Blue Ribbon Sports become the new exclusive distributor of Onitsuka Tigers in the Western U.S. He also requested another shipment of shoes costing $1,000. The shoes came in soon, followed by a letter from an Onitsuka representative confirming that Blue Ribbon Sports would be their partner in the Western U.S. moving forward. Knight quit his accounting job soon after in order to fully commit to Blue Ribbon.

First, he tried selling shoes the standard way, by getting them on the shelves at brick-and-mortar sporting goods stores. Every store owner rejected his samples, citing the lack of demand for yet another track shoe, so Knight thought up a more direct-to-consumer sales method. He traveled the Pacific Northwest in his lime green Plymouth Valiant, going to various track meets and peddling the Tigers to anyone who would have him, from coaches to runners to fans.[192] This method proved more effective than Knight expected, and soon he was running out of shoes to sell. People would write letters asking for the shoes to be delivered by mail, and customers even regularly

---

[191] Knight, Phil. *Shoe Dog: A Memoir by the Creator of Nike*. Reprint edition. Scribner, 2016.
[192] Literary Arts. "Phil Knight Episode - The Archive Project Podcast." Accessed May 9, 2022. https://literary-arts.org/archive/phil-knight/.

showed up to his house to get their hands on a pair. By July, Knight sold out of his first $1,000 shipment, which he'd received just three months prior.

Knight soon went about expanding his territory down the West Coast, taking trips to California in order to sell more shoes at meets. He saved money on travel by sneaking onto military transits headed down the coast, casually hopping on to transport trucks leaving the local air base in his crispest Army uniform. On one trip, at a track meet at Occidental College in Los Angeles, fate would have Knight bump into a man named Jeff Johnson, a friend from Stanford. Johnson was there attending grad school while selling Adidas shoes part time, so Knight attempted to poach some talent from his rivals, asking Johnson to join him at Blue Ribbon Sports. Johnson declined, citing his new marriage needing stability at the moment. Johnson would come to play a role in Nike's story a little further down the line. For now, Knight moved on, continuing to sell Tigers at a steady rate until he hit a speed bump.

One day, Knight received a letter from a man out in Long Island who claimed to be Onitsuka's new exclusive distributor for the entirety of the U.S. Due to this deal, he requested that Knight stop selling the shoes as his sales essentially amounted to poaching. The letter sent Knight into a spiral, eventually culminating in a last-minute trip to Japan to force Onitsuka's executives to talk to him about their arrangement. After meeting with a company rep at his hotel in Kobe, Knight was eventually able to meet Mr. Onitsuka, the company's founder, at Onitsuka headquarters. During the meeting, Mr. Onitsuka told Knight that he reminded him of a younger version of himself. Knight was eventually granted exclusive distribution rights to sell Onitsuka running shoes in the western thirteen states. His new competitor would sell his wrestling shoes nationwide, but would only sell running shoes outside Knight's territory. Knight left happy, his parting gift to the company a $3,500 order for another shipment of Tigers.[193]

Blue Ribbon's first ever hire was Knight's sister, Jeanne. Knight paid her $1.50 an hour to do secretarial work after he found her snooping through his letters to a girlfriend. His second hire, though, came from outside the family. Jeff Johnson, the Stanford classmate he'd reunited with at the Occidental track meet, sent Knight a letter asking to be hired by Blue Ribbon. While he worked weekdays as a social worker, he wanted to work weekends selling Tigers. Johnson quickly alarmed Knight with his passion for the business, sending a flurry of letters up the West Coast with all kinds of different ideas for expanding the company's sales (Knight would call him "the most prolific letter-writer in the history of prolific letter-writers").[194] Knight thought he was unhinged. As Johnson invested more and more time into selling for Blue Ribbon in California, Knight began getting warnings from his banker telling him that, while the company's growth was great, Blue Ribbon's lack of cash balance could lead to problems down the line. This frustrated Knight as he saw no problems with reinvesting profits into growing the business. However, at the same time, Onitsuka was lagging behind in their shipments, slowing the company's momentum. The combination of pressure from his bank and Onitsuka's lack of commitment to their partnership led Knight to take a day job at an accounting firm while still running the company in his spare time.

Luckily, he had two business partners who were also enthusiastic about the business. By this point, Johnson had become fed up with his day job and quit social work completely in order to work for Blue Ribbon full time, growing the company's client list, expanding the business outside the Pacific Northwest and California, and establishing a brick-and-mortar store in Santa Monica. At one point, at the request of a customer,

---

[193] Knight, Phil. *Shoe Dog: A Memoir by the Creator of Nike.* Reprint edition. Scribner, 2016.
[194] Literary Arts. "Phil Knight Episode - The Archive Project Podcast." Accessed May 9, 2022. https://literary-arts.org/archive/phil-knight/.

64

Johnson even modified a pair of Tigers by adding rubber soles from shower slippers to the bottom of the shoe, resulting in a forerunner of the modern running shoe and its thick, arch-supporting midsole.

Bowerman, for his part, was also helping the business along in his own way. Despite having no hand in daily operations, he essentially functioned as Blue Ribbon's main R&D department by continuing his passion for modifying shoes. He experimented extensively with modifying the Tigers for the Oregon track team, and on a trip to Japan for the 1964 Olympics he met with Onitsuka's founder to pitch a new shoe adapted to American runners. While prototypes of the new shoe took quite some time to reach him, the results were perfect: "Soft inner sole, more arch support, heel wedge to reduce stress on the Achilles tendon — they sent the prototype to Bowerman and he went wild for it," remembers Knight.[195] He even went so far as to create a new prototype shoe for Onitsuka to produce. In 1967, Bowerman created a new shoe, a combination of two already-existing Onitsuka running models, made for long distance running. He wanted to name it the "Aztec" as the 1968 Olympics were being held in Mexico City, but Adidas threatened to sue over the name as they already had a shoe named "Azteca Gold". Bowerman went with Cortez, naming it after "that guy who kicked the sh** out of the Aztecs" instead.[196] Bowerman's shoe is an icon and remains a staple of Nike to this day. Tom Hanks wore Cortezes in his character's cross-country run in Forrest Gump, and the shoe has a special place in hip-hop history, with Pulitzer Prize-winning rapper Kendrick Lamar working with Nike to release multiple new versions of it.[197]

---

[195] Knight, Phil. *Shoe Dog: A Memoir by the Creator of Nike*. Reprint edition. Scribner, 2016.
[196] Knight, Phil. *Shoe Dog: A Memoir by the Creator of Nike*. Reprint edition. Scribner, 2016.
[197] Carrillo, Juan. "Origins: What You Didn't Know About The Nike Cortez | Cult Edge," March 24, 2020.
https://cultedge.com/nike-cortez-origins-history/.

Over the next few years, the business continued to grow, doubling its revenue year over year. In 1966, Onitsuka awarded Blue Ribbon a three-year exclusivity deal, securing Knight nationwide distribution rights to the entire U.S. for their track-and-field shoes. The team grew, too: Johnson stepped up to head the company's East Coast operations after some intense deliberations and new key hires were brought in at the suggestion of Bowerman. Knight left his position at Portland State (after meeting his wife-to-be there), and dedicated all his efforts to the company. However, despite its impressive growth trajectory, the company continued to face a few key problems, from both the bank and Onitsuka. Knight's banker, who would loan Blue Ribbon the money to pay for the next shipment of shoes as the last batch was being sold off, continued to be wary of the company's lack of equity. As the size of loans doubled every year, the bank eventually put its foot down, refusing to bankroll the company in 1970 after Knight asked for a $1.2 million loan in anticipation for the doubling of sales from $600,000 in 1969. For their part, Onitsuka continued to be fashionably late on many scheduled shoe deliveries, at one point leaving Blue Ribbon in the lurch for six entire weeks with no shipments of shoes.

In 1970, a shoe seller from the East Coast contacted Knight telling him that he'd been contacted by Onitsuka to become their new exclusive distributor in the U.S. Knight contacted Fujimoto, an Onitsuka employee he'd befriended on a trip to Japan, about this and learned that the company was weighing its options for the future and might drop Blue Ribbon as their U.S. partner in the future. Hearing this, Knight called in his official contact at Onitsuka, Kitami, to meet him in the U.S. to discuss their future together. At their meeting, Kitami stated that "Blue Ribbon sales are disappointing!" and that the company could be tripling its sales each year instead of just doubling them.[198] Eventually, Knight realized that Kitami's trip to the U.S.

---

[198] Knight, Phil. *Shoe Dog: A Memoir by the Creator of Nike*. Reprint edition. Scribner, 2016.

was not just about Blue Ribbon - after stealing a file from his briefcase, he found that the man was there to talk to other U.S. shoe distributors. On their second meeting later that week, Kitami offered Knight a deal: sell a controlling 51% of Blue Ribbon to Onitsuka, or the Japanese company would sign a deal with other U.S. distributors, who they thought could sell more shoes. He left Knight to mull it over.

Worried about Blue Ribbon's future as a company, Knight then went to meet with Nissho Iwai, a multi-billion dollar Japanese trading company. Trading companies like Nissho essentially sold small loans to large volumes of businesses, and high-growth partners like Blue Ribbon were just what they wanted. They'd initially offered to provide loans for Knight's imports of Onitsuka shoes when his deal with the bank fell through, but once Knight learned that the Onitsuka deal was falling apart, the company offered to introduce Knight to other manufacturers in Japan. To test the waters of selling shoes outside of his deal with Onitsuka, Knight signed a contract with a factory used by Adidas in Mexico for 3,000 pairs of soccer shoes, which he planned to sell as American football shoes. The deal technically did not violate Blue Ribbon's agreement with Onitsuka, which stated that he could only import Onitsuka track shoes – it did not mention football or soccer shoes.

Because this new partnership would create an entirely new brand of shoes, the company needed a logo and a name. The new logo was provided by a young artist Knight had met teaching at Portland State named Carolyn Davidson. When she asked what he wanted in the logo, Knight answered "Something that evokes a sense of motion."[199] She came back with what Knight describes as "variations on a single theme, and the theme seemed to be ... fat lightning bolts? Chubby check marks? Morbidly obese squiggles?"[200] While they evoked motion, none of them compelled Knight. Davidson returned a few weeks later with a

---

[199] Knight, Phil. *Shoe Dog: A Memoir by the Creator of Nike*. Reprint edition. Scribner, 2016.
[200] Knight, Phil. *Shoe Dog: A Memoir by the Creator of Nike*. Reprint edition. Scribner, 2016.

new set of designs, and one logo spoke to Knight and Johnson and the rest of the team, one that looked like "a wing," "a whoosh of air," and "something a runner might leave in his or her wake."[201] He paid her 35 dollars for one of the most iconic logos in modern history, at a rate of $2 an hour for 17.5 hours.[202] When the company went public 7 years later, the company paid her 500 Nike shares, which she still owns to this day (now worth over $1 million).[203]

With a new logo finished, the brand still needed a name as the deadline for production drew close. The team came up with two main candidates: Falcon and Dimension Six. Knight preferred the second option as he had made it up himself, but when he asked for opinions, the company couldn't come to a consensus. More names were added to the pot including Bengal and Condor among other animal names, but still none stuck. On the last morning before the company's new shoe line (and all its marketing) was set to drop, the ever-inspired Johnson woke up with a name he found in a dream: Nike, the Greek goddess of victory. A short but impactful name, similar to other iconic brands like Kleenex and Coke. Knight rolled with it.

Unfortunately, Nike's first shoes, produced by the factory in Mexico, turned out to be shoddy at best: "the factory's leather football shoe was pretty, but in cold weather its sole split and cracked," recalls Knight.[204] When a Notre Dame quarterback used the shoe in a game that season, the shoe disintegrated. So, Knight went back to the drawing board with the help of Nissho, the Japanese trading company. Using their contacts, Knight found a factory in Japan called Nippon Rubber which was the perfect partner to produce a new line of Nike shoes. Instead of selling shoes to Japan and giving the remainder to Knight as it

---

[201] Knight, Phil. *Shoe Dog: A Memoir by the Creator of Nike*. Reprint edition. Scribner, 2016.
[202] Literary Arts. "Phil Knight Episode - The Archive Project Podcast." Accessed May 9, 2022. https://literary-arts.org/archive/phil-knight/.
[203] Literary Arts. "Phil Knight Episode - The Archive Project Podcast." Accessed May 9, 2022. https://literary-arts.org/archive/phil-knight/.
[204] Knight, Phil. *Shoe Dog: A Memoir by the Creator of Nike*. Reprint edition. Scribner, 2016.

turned out Onitsuka was doing, the factory would fulfill all his orders. Knight sent over a variety of shoes, including the classic Nike Blazer basketball shoe as well as the Cortez.

The partnership between Nippon Rubber and Nike debuted at the National Sporting Goods Association Show in Chicago in 1972. There, in front of a pyramid of highlighter-orange shoe boxes, more and more sportswear salesmen lined up to get a look at the new brand on the block. Knight scooped up order after order that day, surprising himself and his employees. Onitsuka watched from the sidelines of the show, but Knight knew they would strike soon. Soon after the show, they did just that: Kitami visited Knight in Oregon, handing his lawyer a letter noting that Blue Ribbon's distribution contract with Onitsuka was now void, and also stating that Onitsuka would be suing the company in Japanese court for $16,637.13 in damages. In order to counter the suit, Nike was forced to file its own suit in American court in hopes of beating Onitsuka stateside and pressuring them into withdrawing their case. Besides the lawsuit, the year went relatively well from there on out, with Nike sales growing steadily and a handful of athlete endorsements coming in, but the loss of Onitsuka sales still hurt the company.

By 1974, things were both looking up and coming to a head for Blue Ribbon. The company had raised sales by 50% in 1973, earning $4.8 million by releasing new shoe lines and scoring even more athlete endorsement deals, but the lawsuit with Onitsuka was headed to the courtroom in April. The suit, leveled by Blue Ribbon, alleged that Onitsuka had breached their contract by searching for new U.S. distributors and demanding that Knight sell his controlling stake of Blue Ribbon in order to keep selling Tigers. It also included allegations that Onitsuka had infringed on Blue Ribbon's trademark for their shoes, including the Cortez, by selling the shoes which were registered under Blue Ribbon in the U.S. Blue Ribbon eventually won the case, billing Onitsuka for damages and stopping a lawsuit in Japanese court, but both Blue Ribbon and Onitsuka were allowed by the judge to sell identical shoes, the caveat being that only Blue Ribbon could sell them under their trademarked names.[205]

Divorced fully from Onitsuka, Blue Ribbon headed down a new path as its own brand. As usual, the path forward was not an easy one. In 1974, after the suit was settled, the company's first hurdle popped up: the yen. While the currency had held strong for the first 10 years of Blue Ribbon's trans-Pacific partnership, the Nixon administration divorced the dollar from the gold standard in 1971, breaking the $1-to-¥360 conversion rate that remained after the second World War.[206] By 1974, this change led to fluctuations in the yen's dollar value that changed "like the weather," as well as rising labor costs in Japan. The combination of the two factors worried Knight, so he set off to diversify Blue Ribbon's production facility portfolio. The company looked to set up shop in various different countries but ended up with a factory in Exeter, New Hampshire. To finance retrofitting the factory for Nike production, the company took out a $250,000 loan. Other factories in Taiwan, China, and Vietnam would follow in the decades to come (with their own problems), but the Exeter factory was Nike's first step into the production business.

Year over year, the company continued to grow and change rapidly. By 1976, sales reached $14 million. By 1977, sales almost hit $70 million. In 1979, the company broke the $100 million mark, hitting $140 million. New shoes like the Tailwind (the precursor to the Air Max line) hit the market, bringing in customers with intriguing new technologies, and the company signed deals with bigger and better athletes, including John McEnroe in 1977. In 1978, Blue Ribbon Sports officially became Nike, Inc. Knight had developed a juggernaut, hiring more and

---

[205] Oregonian/OregonLive, Allan Brettman | The. "Attorney Recalls Nike Crossroads Lawsuit." oregonlive, October 9, 2015.
https://www.oregonlive.com/playbooks-profits/2015/10/post_74.html.
[206] Nikkei Asia. "'Nixon Shock' Still Haunts Japan: Ex-Financial Diplomat Gyoten." Accessed May 12, 2022.
https://asia.nikkei.com/Editor-s-Picks/Interview/Nixon-shock-still-haunts-Japan-ex-financial-diplomat-Gyoten.

more accountants and advertisers, but one thing stayed the same from the Blue Ribbon days: a core of dedicated employees, outcasts who had found their niche at Nike and contributed greatly to the company's success. These leaders, including Johnson and other early hires who were brought on at the suggestion of Bowerman, met biannually at retreats they called "Buttfaces." The name was made up by Johnson, who noted at one meeting, "How many multimillion dollar companies can you yell out, 'Hey Buttface,' and the entire management team turns around?"[207] While overseeing a growing company might have been a grueling task at times, these meetings became a source of inspiration for Knight and the rest of management. At the Buttface retreats, the gathered Buttfaces would put their heads together to tackle the company's most pressing problems with smiles on their faces.

It was at one Buttface meeting that Knight brought up the idea of going public. The company was still running high on growth and low on equity, and pressure from the banks loaning Nike the money to finance more shoes was ever-present. On top of that, Knight had a family to think about: his first son, Matthew Knight, was born in 1970, and his second son, Travis, was born in 1973. Knight knew the company needed cash flow for its own sake, and he also knew that his fellow Buttfaces deserved a payout. The company settled on a model which would keep the culture that Knight valued so highly, while also allowing in more public investors to keep the company's coffers lined. Nike would offer a system with two types of stock: class B stocks would be worth one vote a share, while class A stocks would hold more power, with class A holders controlling three quarters of the board of directors. Public investors would get access to class B stock, while the company's inner circle would get access to class A stock — the perfect solution. However, Nike faced one last hurdle before it could IPO: a duty-assessing method called the "American Selling Price"

---

[207] Knight, Phil. *Shoe Dog: A Memoir by the Creator of Nike*. Reprint edition. Scribner, 2016.

Essentially, the American Selling Price (ASP) began as a tool for the U.S. government to protect American industry. The law states that import taxes on nylon shoes (like Nike's) must equal 20% of the shoe's manufacturing cost. However, if there is a "similar shoe" produced in the U.S. to the imported one, the taxes on the imported model must instead equal 20% of the domestic shoe's selling price. American shoemakers, like Converse and Keds, had dusted off the law and put it to use against the upstart Nike brand, selling "similar shoes" to Nike models and marking up their selling prices, resulting in a $25 million fine against Nike for their duties based on the law. Nike could not go public with the $25 million held against them, so they found a way to get around it instead.

First, Nike lobbied Senators to pressure the bureaucrats fining the company. When that didn't prove to be enough, the company created cheap knockoffs of its own shoes in order to drive down their selling price as calculated by the ASP. On top of this, Nike ran ads "telling the story of a little company in Oregon, fighting the big bad government," and, as a final measure, filed its own antitrust lawsuit against the companies who had used the ASP against Nike. The combination of these three blows led the government to ask to settle, with both sides eventually landing on a much more manageable fine of $9 million to Nike. After the fine was paid, Nike went public, making many Buttfaces millionaires overnight while also guaranteeing a more sustainable future for Nike with increased cash flow.

After the IPO, the company continued on its warpath to the top, bolstered by its innovative designs and bold advertising. In 1980, the same year of the IPO, Nike finally brought Knight's "Crazy Idea" to fruition, surpassing Adidas in U.S. market shares.[208] But things didn't stop there: in 1984, Nike took a risk on a basketball player named Michael Jordan, creating a partnership which would exceed the expectations of all parties

---

[208] Banjo, Marc Bain, Shelly. "How Phil Knight Turned the Nike Brand into a Global Powerhouse." Quartz. Accessed May 12, 2022. https://qz.com/442042/more-than-anyone-else-it-was-phil-knight-who-built-nike-from-scratch-into-the-worlds-biggest-sports-brand/.

involved and bringing the running-shoe brand even further into the mainstream.[209] After the multi-billion dollar success of the Jordan signing, more athletes would follow: LeBron James, Tiger Woods, Rafael Nadal, and Cristiano Ronaldo are a few names signed to Nike today, bringing even more prestige to one of the biggest brands in the world.

Knight stepped down as CEO in 2004 following the passing of his eldest son Matthew in a scuba diving accident, and relinquished his role as chairman of the board in 2016, having brought his company to the top of the world.[210] Today, the multi-billionaire gives away $100 million every year to good causes while enjoying retirement with his wife.

---

[209] Badenhausen, Kurt. "Michael Jordan Has Made Over $1 Billion From Nike — The Biggest Endorsement Bargain In Sports." Forbes. Accessed May 12, 2022.
https://www.forbes.com/sites/kurtbadenhausen/2020/05/03/michael-jordans-1-billion-nike-endorsement-is-the-biggest-bargain-in-sports/.
[210] Vinton, Kate. "Nike Cofounder And Chairman Phil Knight Officially Retires From The Board." Forbes. Accessed May 12, 2022.
https://www.forbes.com/sites/katevinton/2016/06/30/nike-cofounder-and-chairman-phil-knight-officially-retires-from-the-board/.

VI.

Chuck Feeney

U.S. Air Force

DFS Group

Chuck Feeney was born one of six children in 1931 in Elizabeth, New Jersey, during the Great Depression. His mother was a nurse, and his father was an insurance underwriter. The Irish Catholic family barely scraped through the Great Depression thanks to their hard work. Chuck was a hustler himself, the kind of kid who shoveled snow, sold Christmas cards, and caddied at golf courses for pocket change, and did what he could to help the family get by. He was a smart but mischievous student, and in the eighth grade was the only student at his middle school to win a scholarship to Regis High School in Manhattan. Despite the school's prestige, Feeney hated the commute and lack of neighborhood friends there. So, he took matters into his own hands. "I got caught cribbing in a religion exam, but it was all part of my plot," he recalls. "If you get caught cribbing in a religious exam, they ask you to leave."[211] And leave, he did – kind of. More specifically, he got himself expelled. Feeney then moved on to attend his neighborhood high school, St. Mary of the Assumption High School in Elizabeth, graduating in June of 1948.

He then volunteered to join the Air Force, knowing full well that he'd eventually be drafted into the military eventually anyway. "I felt, well, I'll just be scratching my ass," he recalls, referring to the U.S.'s post-World War II conscription policy. "I may as well get it over with, so I signed up for three years."[212] He trained as a radio operator for the Air Force at the base in Lackland Air Base near San Antonio, Texas, before being deployed overseas. He ended up working the radios for the U.S. Air Force Radio Squadron's Mobile Detachment 12 at Ashiya Air Base. His squadron operated Signals Intelligence, or SIGINT, a part of the NSA which contributed to breaking Japanese military cyphers towards the end of the Second World War. During his

---

[211] O'Clery, Conor. *The Billionaire Who Wasn't: How Chuck Feeney Secretly Made and Gave Away a Fortune.* 1st edition. PublicAffairs, 2013.
[212] O'Clery, Conor. *The Billionaire Who Wasn't: How Chuck Feeney Secretly Made and Gave Away a Fortune.* 1st edition. PublicAffairs, 2013.

time in post-war Japan, Feeney took the time to expand his skill set, dedicating himself to learning Japanese at a U.S. military language school.

Unfortunately for him, what started as a quiet deployment was interrupted by the Korean War, and his three-year deployment was extended to four years. When the war began in July of 1950, Ashiya Air Base became a staging post for F-80 fighter jets and C-119 transport planes, and Feeney's job became significantly more critical, though he was able to avoid direct combat. He was now tasked with intercepting Russian radio communications from Soviet planes flying around the Sea of Japan, patrolling a border in the sky. Any American planes that flew over the border would be shot down by Russian planes, a lesson that Feeney learned in a very immediate way. One day, a new pilot flew a plane into Russian airspace, and was shot down after five minutes. Aboard the plane were two Russian-language specialists, who Feeney had worked with just a day earlier.

While still in Japan, Feeney began doing research on where he wanted to go using his GI Bill funding. Eventually, Feeney set his eyes on Cornell University's School of Hotel Management. Going to an Ivy League school was a long shot for him, as nobody else in his family had ever attended college, and only one other student from his high school attended college.[213] Luckily, Cornell's School of Hotel Management was the perfect fit – its students had the lowest SAT scores out of all of Cornell's schools, but it also churned out many famous entrepreneurs, including James McLamore and David Edgerton, the co-founders of Burger King, as well as Michael Egan, the military veteran entrepreneur who built up Alamo Rent-A-Car into the giant it is today.[214] After returning home from Japan in July of 1952, Feeney soon received his acceptance letter to the school.

---

[213] Secret Billionaire: The Chuck Feeney Story, 2010. https://www.youtube.com/watch?v=OMcjxe8slYI .

[214] O'Clery, Conor. *The Billionaire Who Wasn't: How Chuck Feeney Secretly Made and Gave Away a Fortune*. 1st edition. PublicAffairs, 2013.

At first, Feeney didn't seem to fit in at Cornell. At the time, most Irish Catholics didn't attend Ivy League schools, and the rest of Cornell looked down on the Hotel School as a whole. Additionally, there was the socio-economic divide: many of his classmates came from money, showing off their shiny cars and bringing family fortunes to the table. "Once they let me in I was certainly capable of competing with the people who were in there," he remembers. "I had to get there to figure that out."[215]

He soon found his entrepreneurial spirit while still going to class, filling in a market left open by Cornell's lack of late-night fast food joints. With no McDonald's available in Ithaca at the time, Feeney noticed that the privileged student body was hungry at night, with a lot of cash to burn. Needing cash as the GI Bill only covered tuition, he started up a small business selling sandwiches to frats and sororities. He would go door to door at night with a basket full of thin-cut sandwiches, making friends and eventually expanding his business with the help of other students to average 700 sandwiches sales a week by his own estimate.[216]

Feeney graduated from Cornell in 1956 with a bachelor's degree in hotel administration. After a brief stint in Los Angeles for the summer, he ended up attending a political science master's program halfway across the world at Grenoble University in France, fulfilling a lifelong dream of traveling to Europe. After completing his master's in eight months, he wound up in Villefranche-sur-Mer, a French resort town that was also home to a rotation of U.S. Navy Sixth Fleet ships.[217] A few people in the town had oriented businesses toward the military presence, but Feeney and an Englishman he met in town came

---

[215] O'Clery, Conor. *The Billionaire Who Wasn't: How Chuck Feeney Secretly Made and Gave Away a Fortune.* 1st edition. PublicAffairs, 2013.

[216] O'Clery, Conor. *The Billionaire Who Wasn't: How Chuck Feeney Secretly Made and Gave Away a Fortune.* 1st edition. PublicAffairs, 2013.

[217] O'Clery, Conor. *The Billionaire Who Wasn't: How Chuck Feeney Secretly Made and Gave Away a Fortune.* 1st edition. PublicAffairs, 2013.

up with a new racket: selling liquor tax-free to be sent to soldiers' home ports in the U.S. A five-pack of spirits in Europe could be sent to the U.S. for a total of $10, while it would cost a whopping $30 stateside – the only thing that their new duty-free buyers needed to do was declare their purchase when they arrived stateside. The model was the perfect scheme for the pair, who were strapped for cash – it required no startup capital and returned cash up front.[218] They made some money off the operation before the Sixth Fleet moved on to Barcelona.

In Barcelona, Feeney connected with another Cornell classmate, Rob Miller. He brought him into the business after Miller quit his job at the Ritz-Carlton. Miller was tired of his desk job, and had heard of duty-free sales from a monk from Hong Kong who he'd met in Barcelona, who told him about the massive duty-free market in his hometown. By 1958, the pair began growing their business in earnest, traveling Europe to sell liquor to American soldiers, and even expanding their inventory to include cameras, trinkets, and perfumes. At one point, Feeney realized that the business could be expanded to sell cheap liquor to tourists, as long as they were from one of the fifteen states that allowed duty-free imports. "I looked at the market and said, if it's good for the military, it must be good for tourists," he recalls. "So we started doing the same thing – selling them gallon packages of liquor."[219]

By 1960, Feeney and Miller had a legitimate setup for their new business. They named the enterprise Tourists International, and opened their offices at a hotel in Lichtenstein. Sales continued to do well, and the business kept growing. Later that year, Feeney came across another American who'd dipped his toes into the world of duty-free sales but failed. Harry Adler had attempted to co-found a perfume-based duty free venture named Duty Free Shoppers, but found himself struggling to gain

---

[218] *Secret Billionaire: The Chuck Feeney Story*, 2010. https://www.youtube.com/watch?v=OMcjxe8slYI.
[219] *Secret Billionaire: The Chuck Feeney Story*, 2010. https://www.youtube.com/watch?v=OMcjxe8slYI.

customers. Feeney scooped up the failing enterprise for $10,000, and hired Adler to join Tourists International.

Around this time, Tourists International expanded into the car business. While aboard Navy ships collecting orders, Feeney and Miller found themselves being asked if they were the duty-free salesmen selling cars. At the time they weren't, but they soon realized that other duty-free businesses were starting to sell entire cars to service members, shipping the tax-free vehicles across the Atlantic at a steep discount – for example, customers could snag a $500 discount on a $1,700 Volkswagen 113 sedan. Like alcohol, shipping cars took no inventory or startup capital, making it a great venture for the pair. They soon founded Cars International as a companion for Tourists International, with multiple offices in Western Germany. They made the rounds with crazy ads for their crazy car deals, and the business made it off the ground despite Europe's growing duty-free competition.

Another Cornell alum joined the fold in 1960. Jeffrey Cornish Mahlstedt was a former customer of Feeney's sandwich business, and was wrapping up his service with the U.S. Seventh Fleet in the Pacific. Feeney had reached out to him about joining Tourists International while he was still on duty, with a focus on opening a wing of the business in Asia. Mahlstedt was discharged from service at the U.S. naval base at Yokosuka, and immediately went about selling duty-free cars to people at the base. He then moved on to Hong Kong, which Feeney and Miller heard was the real duty-free gold mine. On June 23, 1960, Mahlstedt registered Tourist Duty Free Sales Company (Hong Kong) Limited, with him, Feeney, and Miller as its directors. In September of 1960, Miller traveled to Hong Kong to help grow the Asia branch of the business.

Back in the West, Feeney had gone back to the U.S. to meet with a friend (and accountant) from Cornell named Alan Parker about a tax issue. After his businesses were reorganized to solve the tax issue, he learned a key fact about his ventures – they weren't actually making any money. According to Parker (who would go on to own about 20% of DFS Group Ltd.), his audit revealed that "the liabilities exceeded the assets by approximately $1,600,000."[220]

"Cash flow was tremendous," Parker recalls, "and people paid very early for the cars, so everybody looked at this money in the bank as profit, as it were. There were no expense controls of any sort, people spent money as they saw fit, and it resulted in an enormous deficit. We would be very lucky if we just got it out of debt and closed it down, and moved on to something else."[221]

While the business floundered, Feeney was soon able to find a way out. At the time, duty free shops at airports were only able to operate through government contracts sold to the highest bidder.[222] Feeney secured a concession to open a duty-free shop at Honolulu International Airport to the tune of $125,000 over 5 years. With international travel becoming a growing phenomenon at the time, the shop began raking in cash, providing a stable income to help Tourists International dig itself out of its hole. The company's Hong Kong branch soon followed suit, securing the first duty-free stand at Kai Tak International Airport in Hong Kong. While these two concessions provided some stable income to the company, Feeney had his sights set on larger enterprises.

His idea was to piggyback off of Duty Free Shoppers, the failed business which he'd bought out for $10,000. The concept behind Duty Free Shoppers (DFS) was essentially setting up a network of shops in various countries carrying samples of goods (mostly alcohol) for sale, but no actual inventory. The goods shown in the shops wouldn't be limited to those produced in the local country, but anywhere within the DFS network – a buyer in Canada could get 5 bottles of Johnny Walker from Amsterdam sent to his home in America by just filling out a customs form and sending it to Europe. Tourists International began setting up

---

[220] *Secret Billionaire: The Chuck Feeney Story*, 2010. https://www.youtube.com/watch?v=OMcjxe8slYI.
[221] *Secret Billionaire: The Chuck Feeney Story*, 2010. https://www.youtube.com/watch?v=OMcjxe8slYI.
[222] *Secret Billionaire: The Chuck Feeney Story*, 2010. https://www.youtube.com/watch?v=OMcjxe8slYI.

a network of these shops in Canada and Mexico near their respective U.S. borders, and the shops quickly began pulling in "a gigantic amount of profit."[223]

By 1964, business was in full swing for Tourists and Cars International. The company was operating in 27 countries, with over 200 employees. Unfortunately, a slowdown was on the horizon. Both competition and new regulations contributed to this, with more companies entering the duty-free car sales space, while the U.S. government cut down on citizens' right to import duty-free alcohol from five bottles to just one. These changes spelled huge losses for Feeney's businesses, eventually forcing him to fold Tourists International and Cars International into a single business, this under the name Duty Free Shoppers. DFS shifted focus away from the weakened car and liquor models, instead shifting to its foothold in the retail market as established by its stores in the Hong Kong and Honolulu airports.

Luckily for DFS, their turn to duty-free shops in airports came at just the right time – Japan was beginning to allow its citizens to travel abroad after a travel ban aimed at healing its shattered post-war economy. Many Japanese tourists headed to Honolulu, where they were amazed at the cheap prices for alcohol and cigarettes on display at DFS' airport shop. The Hong Kong shop found itself similarly inundated with Japanese tourist dollars, and DFS soon opened larger retail spaces in both Waikiki and Hong Kong to meet their increasing demand.

By 1969, business hit full stride for DFS. Feeney was regularly mingling with Hong Kong's British upper set, with yacht parties and black-tie dinners becoming a normal occurrence for him and his growing family. At the same time, Feeney was becoming disillusioned with his new lifestyle, which was far from the close-knit community he'd known in New Jersey. So, he suggested to Miller that DFS should give 5% of its pre-tax profits to charities. Miller was still infatuated with his

---

[223] O'Clery, Conor. *The Billionaire Who Wasn't: How Chuck Feeney Secretly Made and Gave Away a Fortune.* 1st edition. PublicAffairs, 2013.

upper-class lifestyle and didn't understand where Feeney was coming from, but he agreed with the change anyway.

DFS continued to grow throughout the 1970's, establishing new branches in the Pacific and North America. Feeney, who owned 38.75% of DFS at the time, took home $18 million in dividends in 1978, which rose to $23 million by 1980. Luckily for charities around the world, he was beginning to tire of his money. "I am not really into money," he told a reporter from Pacific Business News in 1980. "Some people get their kicks that way. That's not my style."[224] His definition of happiness, having made millions of dollars, was not about the money. "There has to be a balance in life," he said. "A balance of business, family, and the opportunity to learn and teach."[225] This mindset stemmed, in part, from Andrew Carnegie's essay, Wealth. In it, Carnegie argues that "that the best means of benefiting the community is to place within its reach the ladders upon which the aspiring can rise."[226] Carnegie urged his reader to give money to various causes across society, including the arts, parks, and public institutions, and to give that money while one was still living. "I do remember somebody gave me a copy of a speech Carnegie had given at Cornell, and for some reason I researched that speech and read two books on Carnegie," Feeney recalls.[227] He also learned about charity from various religions, many of which preach that acts of charity without public announcement is the highest form of giving.

Feeney decided to set up a charity in Bermuda, planning to gift large amounts of money to various causes around the

---

[224] O'Clery, Conor. *The Billionaire Who Wasn't: How Chuck Feeney Secretly Made and Gave Away a Fortune*. 1st edition. PublicAffairs, 2013.
[225] O'Clery, Conor. *The Billionaire Who Wasn't: How Chuck Feeney Secretly Made and Gave Away a Fortune*. 1st edition. PublicAffairs, 2013.
[226] York, Carnegie Corporation of New. "The Gospel of Wealth." Carnegie Corporation of New York. Accessed January 26, 2023. https://www.carnegie.org/about/our-history/gospelofwealth/.
[227] O'Clery, Conor. *The Billionaire Who Wasn't: How Chuck Feeney Secretly Made and Gave Away a Fortune*. 1st edition. PublicAffairs, 2013.

world. Working out of Bermuda allowed him to operate with lower taxes and with more anonymity – the small British territory didn't tax personal income, corporate income, or charities, and also allowed the establishment of foundations without public disclosure. Unfortunately for his kids, the family would have to reside in the territory for a full year before Feeney was able to start his foundation. The family moved into a large villa on the island, and Feeney started his first venture into charity, named the Davney Fund. The fund, while not a foundation, distributed $1 million of Feeney's money to help deserving students pay for college, also funding the children of DFS employees and other people who'd helped Feeney along the way. Feeney also made his first big individual act of charity in 1981, donating a check of over $700,000 to Cornell.

Later that same year, Feeney began the process of starting the Atlantic Foundation, which would eventually become the Atlantic Philanthropies – the organization which would help Feeney give away all his wealth. To found the charity, Feeney had to navigate Bermuda's narrow interpretation of what a charitable organization actually was. For example, the government didn't see donations to sports organizations as charitable activities, and Feeney was a great fan of many sports. So, he hired an English law firm to help him draft legislation to establish a unique charity with special powers within Bermuda: he wanted the organization to donate anonymously, operate worldwide, and also run its own businesses, all of which would require a special act by Bermuda's parliament. By 1982, the House of Assembly approved the Atlantic Foundation Company Act, which established the Atlantic Foundation with some concessions in place – in order to prove to parliament that the charity would be the real deal, the bill allowed the Bermuda Charity Commissioners to oversee all of its operations. On March 1, 1982, the Atlantic Foundation began operation with an initial budget of $5 million and the declared goal of helping projects focused on relieving poverty and suffering, advancing education, and supporting the causes of health, youth, old age, and international justice.[228] After the charity's founding, Feeney handed out copies of Carnegie's Wealth to everyone working on the project. This was when they realized that he was dead set on giving away almost all his wealth, besides a fund set aside for his wife Danielle and their children. They also signed binding confidentiality agreements as part of Feeney's dedication to anonymity – both out of principle, and to avoid the possibility of bad press coming his way.

Back on the business side of things, DFS was still printing money for its owners, though they'd grown increasingly distant from each other on a personal level over the years. The firm stayed ahead of the market as tourism boomed, thanks to its solid understanding of the industry. DFS invested heavily into analysis, researching which places Japanese tourists would flock to next, but also leaned on its owners' expertise to keep up its network of duty-free shops in airports around the world. Those shops were put up to bid every few years, and DFS leadership needed to get their bid amounts right to keep hold of their empire. In the early 1980's, DFS used its finances to outbid a series of competitors in airports around the Pacific, securing its future in Guam, Hawaii, and Alaska for the next decade.

By 1984, Feeney was ready to fully commit his wealth to the Atlantic Foundation. Over the two years following the establishment of the Atlantic Foundation, the organization had channeled a full $14 million into Cornell On November 23, 1984, he sold his 38.75% stake in DFS to the Atlantic Foundation for a huge sum, which was hard to calculate due to its illiquid nature. Estimates range from $500 million to almost $1 billion, rivaling the capital of banking firms like Bear Stearns and Morgan Stanley at the time.

Feeney split his time between his charity and his various business ventures, some of which he operated outside of DFS. As for his main company, DFS became the world's largest liquor retailer by 1986, selling $250 million in drinks every year. It was

---

[228] O'Clery, Conor. *The Billionaire Who Wasn't: How Chuck Feeney Secretly Made and Gave Away a Fortune.* 1st edition. PublicAffairs, 2013.

also the largest single retailer in various places around the Pacific. Despite this business empire, Feeney and his partners operated in relative anonymity until 1988, when Forbes placed him on their list of the 400 richest Americans. Feeney almost topped out the list at number 23, with an estimated net worth of $1.3 billion – unfortunately for the magazine (and Feeney), they didn't realize that almost all his wealth had been transferred to the Atlantic Foundation.

As the 1990's went on, Feeney began looking to pull out of DFS. The Gulf War had shown the volatility of a business reliant on tourism, and money from Japanese tourists had begun slowing down even as tourism bounced back after the conflict. Another motivating factor was the freedom that comes with liquid assets in one's bank account. He tried to convince his business partners to buy into the idea, which took a full two years to do. After much deliberation, the majority of DFS was eventually sold off to luxury conglomerate LVMH, for the price of $2.47 billion – $1.6 billion of which went to Feeney and his charity.[229]

The Atlantic Foundation and the Atlantic Trust, its U.S.-based arm, had paid out $122 million in gifts in the seven years leading up to 1991.[230] The foundation operated very meticulously, conducting in-depth research into all of its donation recipients. Feeney himself would go to sites where his charity was planning to give grants, talking to people and making sure that their projects were the best recipients possible. Atlantic contributed to projects in many underappreciated areas, including funding education in the Republic of Ireland and

---

[229] Miller, Judith. "He Gave Away $600 Million, and No One Knew." *The New York Times*, January 23, 1997, sec. New York.
https://www.nytimes.com/1997/01/23/nyregion/he-gave-away-600-million-and-no-one-knew.html.

[230] O'Clery, Conor. *The Billionaire Who Wasn't: How Chuck Feeney Secretly Made and Gave Away a Fortune.* 1st edition. PublicAffairs, 2013.

Australia, buying HIV/AIDS medication for people in South Africa, and working on Vietnam's healthcare system.[231]

With the sale of DFS to LVMH, Feeney realized that his secret life as a philanthropist would soon be revealed. To preempt this, he went to the New York Times with a juicy story promoting his charity's dedication to philanthropy. The story marked a massive shift in his operation, but the new funds from DFS' sale and the press from the story gave new power to his organization, in the form of a powerful following – including people like Bill Gates and Warren Buffett.

After the sale, Feeney was able to fully focus on his charities. He created a game plan for his organization, with the stated goal of giving in 5 different sectors: aging, children and youth, population health, reconciliation and human rights, and any initiatives chosen by the Founding Chair. Since the foundation's beginning in 1982, it's given over $8 billion to causes across the globe, including the aforementioned programs in Ireland, Australia, South Africa, and Vietnam. Other beneficiaries include bridge-building efforts in Cuba, the University of California, San Francisco, and the Global Brain Health Institute (an organization dedicated to ending dementia), and Operation Smile (which directly funds cleft-palate surgeries around the globe).[232, 233] In 2002, the Atlantic Philanthropies announced that the charity would become a limited-life foundation, meaning that it would close operations after fully

---

[231] The Atlantic Philanthropies. "Chuck Feeney's Story – Intro." Accessed January 12, 2023.
https://www.atlanticphilanthropies.org/chuck-feeneys-story.
[232] The Atlantic Philanthropies. "Chuck Feeney's Story – Chapter 2." Accessed January 27, 2023.
https://www.atlanticphilanthropies.org/chuck-feeneys-story/chuck-feeneys-story-chapter-2.
[233] Bertoni, Steven. "Chuck Feeney: The Billionaire Who Is Trying To Go Broke." Forbes. Accessed January 12, 2023.
https://www.forbes.com/sites/stevenbertoni/2012/09/18/chuck-feeney-the-billionaire-who-is-trying-to-go-broke/.

dispersing all its funds.[234] The last gift of the charity, given in 2017, was a sort of bookend for the whole operation: just like its first donation, Feeney's foundation gave its last $7 million to Cornell University, one of its biggest recipients over the course of its lifetime. Feeney, now 91, was last noted to have a net worth of $2 million and was living in a rented San Francisco apartment at the time of the gift. "You're always nervous handling so much money, but we seem to have worked it pretty well," he told the New York Times in an interview following the donation.

---

[234] West, Melanie Grayce. "Atlantic Philanthropies Announces $200 Million in Two Gifts." *Wall Street Journal,* June 1, 2016, sec. US. http://www.wsj.com/articles/atlantic-philanthropies-announces-200-million-in-two-gifts-1464739471.

VII.

Berry Gordy, Jr.

U.S. Army

Motown Records

With artists like Marvin Gaye, The Jackson 5, and Stevie Wonder, Motown Records has left an indelible mark on the American music industry from the 1960s to today. The label played a massive role in racially integrating the music business by combining its soul-based sound with pop sensibilities, propelling Black artists into the mainstream during a time of racial tensions. From the late 1960s until just before its sale in the 1980s, the label was the largest Black-owned business in the country, and by the 1990s it would be valued at a whopping $301 million in another sale.[235] Motown defined genres while also providing inspiration to generations of artists and entrepreneurs to this day.

The label was founded by Berry Gordy III, also known as Berry Gordy Jr. Born on November 28, 1929 in Detroit, Michigan, Gordy was the seventh of eight children born to Berry "Pop" Gordy Sr. and his wife Bertha Fuller Gordy.[236] His family was (eventually) middle-class and hard-working, with both his mother and father starting numerous businesses. Pop Gordy ran multiple businesses over the years, including a grocery store and a contracting business, while Bertha started her own insurance agency and supported other family ventures.[237] From a young age, the eight Gordy children were taught the value of hard work and entrepreneurship as they all pitched in to help the family enterprises. As Gordy Jr. grew through his childhood years during the Great Depression, Pop Gordy worked up to four jobs at once in order to provide a comfortable life for the entire clan.[238] At one point, the family of ten shared just four beds

---

[235] Bates, J. (1988, June 29). *Berry Gordy Sells Motown Records for $61 Million*. Los Angeles Times.
https://www.latimes.com/archives/la-xpm-1988-06-29-fi-4916-story.html
[236] *Berry Gordy | Motown Museum | Home of Hitsville U.S.A.* (n.d.). Motown Museum. Retrieved August 3, 2022, from
https://www.motownmuseum.org/legacy/berry-gordy/
[237] *Berry Gordy | Motown Museum | Home of Hitsville U.S.A.* (n.d.). Motown Museum. Retrieved August 3, 2022, from
https://www.motownmuseum.org/legacy/berry-gordy/
[238] Gordy, B. (2013). *To Be Loved: The Music, the Magic, the Memories of Motown*. RosettaBooks.

amongst themselves, forced to stay in a "small two-story shacklike house" that Pop Gordy had fixed up in exchange for lower rent.[239] There, while also collecting welfare to supplement the large family's small income, they fought a constant battle against a rat infestation until they gained financial stability, moving to a townhouse in Detroit's Eastside.[240]

Besides growing up with economic struggles in the face of the largest financial crisis of the century, Gordy also grew up in a racially divided America. His grandfather, the first Berry Gordy, was born a slave, the son of a slave woman and her white owner.[241] Even after abolition, he worked the land much like a slave. He would go on to have twenty-three children with his wife, of which only nine survived. One of those nine was Pop Gordy, a country boy who, after serving his country in World War I, moved to Detroit and began slowly building his way to a stable middle-class lifestyle for himself and his growing family.[242] From early on in his life, the youngest Gordy faced racial discrimination in school from white classmates while he watched his Black peers make self-deprecating jokes about their own skin color. His white teachers only read their students stories like Snow White and Cinderella (though Little Black Sambo somehow made the reading list), and in the movie theaters, Black actors only portrayed "caricatures who made up the comedy relief: bulging eyes and bobbing heads – that they were always scratching," Gordy remembered.[243]

Overall, young Gordy had just one hero who looked like him – famous boxer Joe Louis. "Whenever Joe Louis fought it was a holiday for black folks," he recalled, but when Louis

---

[239] Gordy, B. (2013). *To Be Loved: The Music, the Magic, the Memories of Motown*. RosettaBooks.
[240] Gordy, B. (2013). *To Be Loved: The Music, the Magic, the Memories of Motown*. RosettaBooks.
[241] Gordy, B. (2013). *To Be Loved: The Music, the Magic, the Memories of Motown*. RosettaBooks.
[242] Gordy, B. (2013). *To Be Loved: The Music, the Magic, the Memories of Motown*. RosettaBooks.
[243] Gordy, B. (2013). *To Be Loved: The Music, the Magic, the Memories of Motown*. RosettaBooks.

defeated Max Schmeling of Nazi Germany, Gordy saw his hero become the man of the hour for his whole country, showing him that such a thing was possible even for a Black man decades before the Civil Rights Movement found its success.[244] Of course, there were also musicians like Nat King Cole and Billy Eckstine who were stars in their own right, but none matched up to Louis in Gordy's eyes. Uncle B.A., his mother's brother, tried to teach Gordy piano from a young age, and he began to enjoy composing his own songs with the basic chords taught to him. However, after the Louis-Schmeling fight, boxing began taking up more of Gordy's attention, especially as he began trying to hit it off with the ladies.

Gordy started boxing at the Brewster Center, a local Detroit recreation center near his house. After getting beat up in his first fight, Gordy quickly flew up the ranks in his weight class (just 112 pounds), eventually making his amateur debut as he entered the tenth grade.[245] He put in the hard work necessary to become a good boxer, hitting the gym at 5:30 every morning while also swearing off drinking, smoking, and girls. However, he kept up his affair with music, taking music lessons and learning how to sing until he decided to put music to the side and fully commit to boxing – he quit school in the eleventh grade to go pro in the ring. On November 19, 1948, Gordy fought on the same card as Joe Louis, his hero, winning his first match by decision.[246] He went on to gain weight and move up to the featherweight division, winning ten of his fifteen bouts, while hoping for a shot at a title sometime in the future.

Unfortunately for his boxing career, Gordy was a strong boxer but never attained a particularly high ranking, meaning upper-echelon boxers had little incentive to fight him. Eventually realizing the unstable nature of a career in boxing, Gordy decided

---

[244] Gordy, B. (2013). *To Be Loved: The Music, the Magic, the Memories of Motown*. RosettaBooks.
[245] Gordy, B. (2013). *To Be Loved: The Music, the Magic, the Memories of Motown*. RosettaBooks.
[246] Gordy, B. (2013). *To Be Loved: The Music, the Magic, the Memories of Motown*. RosettaBooks.

to turn back to music instead when he saw a poster for a Battle of the Bands event next to an ad for a boxing match: "I stared at both posters for some time, realizing the fighters could fight once and maybe not fight again for three or four weeks, or months, or never. The bands were doing it every night, city after city, and not getting hurt. I then noticed the fighters were about twenty-three and looked fifty; the band leaders about fifty and looked twenty-three."[247] He committed fully to his new career in songwriting, writing a jingle for his family's print shop which actually helped the shop pick up more business after the ad aired on local radio. Unfortunately for Gordy's budding songwriting career, though, the Korean War called, and he was asked to report to Fort Custer to fight for Uncle Sam at age twenty-two.[248]

From Fort Custer, Gordy moved to Camp Chaffee, Arkansas, for basic training. He had tried to dodge the draft by answering questions on the IQ test incorrectly at Fort Custer, but he passed anyway and was accepted into service. At first, Gordy applied for Special Services (the branch of the Army that entertained the troops) so he could employ his skills as a class clown and entertainer while also avoiding combat, but he lacked the resume. Instead, he was sent to leadership school, where he excelled. From there, Gordy was sent across the Pacific Ocean to serve with the 58th Field Artillery Battalion, 3rd Infantry Division near Panmunjom, South Korea.[249] In Korea, his unit was stationed just behind the front-line infantry, with soldiers being called to the front lines whenever backup was needed. Luckily for his life, Gordy was able to snag a job as a chaplain's assistant, playing the organ and driving his Jeep to and from services. His elation at getting a safer job was short lived, though, as he learned that the chaplain was delivering service to front-line

---

[247] Gordy, B. (2013). *To Be Loved: The Music, the Magic, the Memories of Motown*. RosettaBooks.
[248] Gordy, B. (2013). *To Be Loved: The Music, the Magic, the Memories of Motown*. RosettaBooks.
[249] *Berry Gordy's Biography*. (n.d.). The HistoryMakers. Retrieved August 3, 2022, from https://www.thehistorymakers.org/biography/berry-gordy

troops. Driving back and forth from the front, Gordy saw the faces of the other young men sent to fight in Korea, which made him appreciate his position even more. While he was only on the front lines as almost a day job, they had to live the war fully. "I will never forget the terrified look on those young faces walking into the unknown while I was driving away," he remembers.[250] He made his way out of Korea unscathed and returned to Detroit in 1953.

Back home, Gordy decided to open a record shop with a friend from the military. With the help of his brother and father's bank accounts, Gordy opened the 3D Record Mart – House of Jazz.[251] Unfortunately for him, most of his urban clientele weren't interested in the records of Miles Davis or Charlie Parker. Instead, they wanted the store to stock more Blues records, which were hotter at the time. While Gordy eventually realized that "the customer is always right" and began stocking Blues records, the change came too late – the store went under, and he wasted his family's investments because he'd refused to change with the times. The one win he'd take away from the failed venture was a healthy respect for Blues music and the importance of making music relatable to the common person.

Humbled by the failure of the 3D Record Mart, Gordy resorted to more traditional means to make ends meet. He'd met a woman, Thelma Coleman, and wanted to start a family with her. To support his loved ones Gordy worked as a salesman for a cookware company, selling sets of pots and pans for hundreds of dollars to make a living.[252] One day, he took his father on a sales call to a poor family to close a deal, and sold the man a full set of cookware for $272. After the sale, his father dressed him down outside. He told Gordy that, while his sales techniques were great, what he was doing was unethical. The family could not

---

[250] Gordy, B. (2013). *To Be Loved: The Music, the Magic, the Memories of Motown*. RosettaBooks.
[251] Gordy, B. (2013). *To Be Loved: The Music, the Magic, the Memories of Motown*. RosettaBooks.
[252] Gordy, B. (2013). *To Be Loved: The Music, the Magic, the Memories of Motown*. RosettaBooks.

afford the cookware, and Gordy had exploited the father wanting the best for his family to bait him into making a purchase he couldn't afford. Ashamed, Gordy quit the sales business and turned to songwriting for a time, before realizing that the business wasn't consistent enough to provide for his growing family of four. He took an assembly-line job at a Lincoln-Mercury factory, paying the bills with his day job while continuing to write songs on the side.

Gordy worked at the Lincoln-Mercury plant for two years before his long-standing affair with music pulled him away from the nine-to-five lifestyle. One day at the factory, his older coworkers were counting down the days to their retirement when he realized that he would have to work thirty-three more years until he could be freed from the daily grind. Wanting to live his life true to himself, Gordy quit the plant soon after, buying himself a new silk suit and haircut to look the part of a songwriter. His wife and in-laws were not impressed.

In early 1957, when Gordy fully committed to songwriting, music was everywhere in Detroit. "People were singing on street corners, in barber shops, nightclubs, the churches, the movies, on the radio, everywhere," he recalls.[253] Luckily for Gordy, two of his sisters, Gwen and Anna, worked at one of Detroit's biggest clubs, the Flame Show Bar, and were well-loved by clientele and performers alike. Gordy's first big break into the music industry came one night at the Flame, when Gwen introduced him to Al Green, a manager who owned the club and had signed a few artists to his own publishing company. With a foot in the door, Gordy rushed to Green's label Pearl Music Company the next day and began writing songs with a man named Roquel Billy Davis. Together, they began writing songs for Al Green's artists, including up-and-comer Jackie Wilson. The trio scored their first hit with "Reet Petite," which

---

[253] Gordy, B. (2013). *To Be Loved: The Music, the Magic, the Memories of Motown*. RosettaBooks.

succeeded in both the U.S. and U.K. (it would go on to peak at number one on the U.K. Billboard charts after Wilson's death).[254]

Gordy and Davis parlayed their success with Wilson into working with other artists through the Pearl Music label. Gordy's next big collaboration was with William "Smokey" Robinson, who he helped teach the art of songwriting, going through hundreds of drafts with the young artist before he made his debut on his eighteenth birthday with "Got a Job."[255] As Gordy continued to write hits with Jackie Wilson like "To Be Loved" and "Lonely Teardrops", he realized that, for all his efforts writing chart-toppers for the star, he wasn't getting the credit he deserved. In his autobiography *To Be Loved*, he remembered, "I had sometimes felt like Cyrano de Bergerac, knowing that my words and feelings had gone into the love songs that Jackie sang to seduce all those women who wouldn't give me a second thought."[256] Additionally, he realized that the other songwriters on Wilson's albums were making just as much as he was despite the fact that their songs were all B-sides while his were topping the charts.[257] These songwriters were the family members of label executives. Wanting more money for his successes, he gave his label an ultimatum: he wanted to write for the B-sides of albums as well, essentially telling the label to buzz off with the blatant nepotism. The label rejected the ultimatum and Gordy was out as a songwriter for Wilson, despite writing five back-to-back hits for the star.

With no stable job writing songs for the label anymore, Gordy was stuck. His sister Gwen and his partner Davis, who'd both left the label with him, wanted to start their own label but Gordy wanted to do his own thing instead. He began managing

---

[254] *British Hit Singles & Albums.* (2021). In *Wikipedia.* https://en.wikipedia.org/w/index.php?title=British_Hit_Singles_%26_Albums&oldid=1047171384

[255] Gordy, B. (2013). *To Be Loved: The Music, the Magic, the Memories of Motown.* RosettaBooks.

[256] Gordy, B. (2013). *To Be Loved: The Music, the Magic, the Memories of Motown.* RosettaBooks.

[257] Gordy, B. (2013). *To Be Loved: The Music, the Magic, the Memories of Motown.* RosettaBooks.

Smokey Robinson and his band The Miracles as their debut record started to take off in Detroit.[258] Wanting to make more from his music career, Gordy tried going into producing and publishing, but quickly moved on from that and decided to create his own record label. He named it Tamla after "Tammy" by Debbie Reynolds, the number one pop record at the time.[259] Because he lacked a steady job at the time, Gordy turned to his family for support, negotiating a seed round of $800 from the Ber-Berry Co-op, his family's savings fund.[260] Remembering his failed venture with the 3D Record Mart, the family forced him to pledge a portion of his future royalties as a security for the loan.[261]

Smokey Robinson and The Miracles were the label's first artists, but Tamla's first big record, "Come To Me," was a song by Marv Johnson, written by him and Gordy. The national distribution of the record was handled by United Artists, making it the first hit single of the entertainment company's record division, which usually dealt in movie soundtracks.[262] The single's success brought fame and money to Gordy as the label owner, allowing him to grow his partnership with United Artists and bringing more artists to his doorstep. Soon after Johnson's "Come To Me," the Miracles released "Bad Girl" with Gordy's other record label, Motown. The initial plan was to release solo artist records under the Tamla label, while groups like The Miracles would be under Motown. Off the back of their hit record, The Miracles went to perform at the Apollo in Harlem, the same stage where many of their idols performed before them.

---

[258] Gordy, B. (2013). *To Be Loved: The Music, the Magic, the Memories of Motown*. RosettaBooks.
[259] Gordy, B. (2013). *To Be Loved: The Music, the Magic, the Memories of Motown*. RosettaBooks.
[260] *Berry Gordy | Motown Museum | Home of Hitsville U.S.A.* (n.d.). Motown Museum. Retrieved August 3, 2022, from
https://www.motownmuseum.org/legacy/berry-gordy/
[261] Gordy, B. (2013). *To Be Loved: The Music, the Magic, the Memories of Motown*. RosettaBooks.
[262] Gordy, B. (2013). *To Be Loved: The Music, the Magic, the Memories of Motown*. RosettaBooks.

More and more artists and musicians flocked to Gordy, and by 1959, he opened up shop on 2648 West Grand Boulevard, housing his family in the upper unit while the garage became a recording studio.[263] Outside above the picture window on the first floor was a massive sign that read, "Hitsville, U.S.A."

Hitsville would continue pumping out hits, like Barrett Strong's "Money (That's What I Want)" (which would later be performed by the Beatles and Rolling Stones), while even more artists were drawn to the label. By 1960, Smokey Robinson's "Shop Around" became the label's first million-sale record, and the Tamla and Motown labels were incorporated under the Motown Record Corporation that same year.[264] The label continued to grow thanks to its focus on quality – during their weekly song-pitching meetings, the bar for success became: "If you had a dollar, would you buy this record, or buy a sandwich?"[265] With this focus, the label became a hitmaking machine thanks to Gordy's tight control combined with a culture of competition within the label. Marvin Gaye once referred to the company as "the Gestapo. It was a loving Gestapo – because Berry is a loving cat – but it was still the Gestapo."[266] On top of competing during songwriting sessions, artists were taught how to hold themselves in society as well as how to perform on stage. The Miracles had had a disastrous first performance at the Apollo, and Gordy would have none of that going forward –

---

[263] *Berry Gordy | Motown Museum | Home of Hitsville U.S.A.* (n.d.). Motown Museum. Retrieved August 3, 2022, from
https://www.motownmuseum.org/legacy/berry-gordy/
[264] Brown, M. (2016, January 19). Berry Gordy: The man who built Motown.
https://s.telegraph.co.uk/graphics/projects/berry-gordy-motown/index.html
[265] Brown, M. (2016, January 19). *Berry Gordy: The man who built Motown.*
https://s.telegraph.co.uk/graphics/projects/berry-gordy-motown/index.html
[266] Brown, M. (2016, January 19). Berry Gordy: The man who built Motown.
https://s.telegraph.co.uk/graphics/projects/berry-gordy-motown/index.html

artists were guided by Maxine Powell's Artist Development department, and in-house choreographer Cholly Atkins taught groups like The Temptations their signature tight choreography.[267]

The hits would not stop over the next decade. Diana Ross and The Supremes, The Temptations, Marvin Gaye, Gladys Knight and The Pips, Stevie Wonder, and The Jackson 5 all came through the Hitsville doors between 1960 and 1971, supported by Gordy's handpicked cast of songwriters, producers, and staff. The label racked up twenty-one Billboard number one hits over that timespan, spending a collective sixty-two weeks at the top of the charts.[268] That level of success would be impressive for any independent label, but for a Black-owned and operated label to have that kind of success when companies were hesitant to even hire Black models in commercials was unheard of.[269]

Eventually, though, all good things must end, or at least change. Wanting to expand beyond just music and into entertainment, Gordy moved the business to Los Angeles in 1972. There, Diana Ross starred in Lady Sings the Blues and Mahogany, while Gordy moved on from Motown Records to lead Motown Industries, a new umbrella company formed to include his interest in entertainment.[270] While Motown Industries found success with films, television shows, and even Broadway musicals, the record label began to slow down as the sounds of the times moved past it. Some stars like Stevie Wonder and Marvin Gaye wanted more power over their artistic process,

---

[267] Brown, M. (2016, January 19). Berry Gordy: The man who built Motown.
https://s.telegraph.co.uk/graphics/projects/berry-gordy-motown/index.html
[268] Motown discography. (2022). In *Wikipedia*.
https://en.wikipedia.org/w/index.php?title=Motown_discography&oldid=1091162228
[269] Brown, M. (2016, January 19). *Berry Gordy: The man who built Motown.*
https://s.telegraph.co.uk/graphics/projects/berry-gordy-motown/index.html
[270] *Berry Gordy.* (n.d.). Entrepreneur. Retrieved August 3, 2022, from
https://www.entrepreneur.com/article/197634

while Diana Ross was poached by RCA to the tune of $20 million.

In 1988, Gordy sold Motown Records to MCA Records and Boston Ventures for $61 million. Later that year, he was inducted into the Rock and Roll Hall of Fame. He continued to have a hand in Motown's affairs for a long time after the sale, helping write songs and produce songs until 2019, when he announced his full retirement from the entertainment industry at age 89. He is still involved with Motown, having helped to establish the $50 million expansion to the Motown Museum in Detroit, located at the original Hitsville location on 2648 West Grand.[271]

---

[271] *Berry Gordy*. (n.d.). Entrepreneur. Retrieved August 3, 2022, from https://www.entrepreneur.com/article/197634

VIII.

Vincent Viola

U.S. Army

Virtu Financial

Vincent Viola was born in Brooklyn, New York, in 1956 to Virginia and John A. Viola. Looking back, he described Williamsburg, the community he grew up in, as "a very, very parochial, if not insulated, Italian-American neighborhood."[272] Growing up, most of the men in his life had also served in the military in World War II, which would later influence Viola's to join the military.

"Europe, Pacific, the Army Air Corps, Army Infantry, support soldiers – so on both sides of my family, we had Bronze Star winners, CIB recipients, too, navigators, bombardiers on B17s, and many, many missions. So this family pulsed with a patriotic sense of duty to this country that gave us a great life," he recalls.[273] The family's military history went even further back than World War II, though. His grandfather, who brought his father's side of the family to America from Italy's Campania region, actually served as a noncommissioned officer in the Italian Army for 14 years, seeing action in a prestigious artillery unit during World War I.

Despite his family's long line of military service, Viola's path to the military wasn't as clear as you'd assume. He graduated high school as the Vietnam War was close to reaching its end and anti-war fervor was hitting its stride. "The socialization of the anti-military and anti-war movement had trickled from the campuses to the high school hallways by the time – 1969, '70, '71 – that period. And much like the gestalt of popular culture takes root, and it is least commonly denominated, people would just almost organically attract to antiwar protests. A few had very committed, intellectually grounded reasons for participating in these protests. Many just did it almost as a social activity. Maybe because my family had

---

[272] The West Point Center For Oral History. "USMA Class of 1977: The Honor Scandal and Beyond." Accessed August 30, 2023.
https://www.westpointcoh.org/interviews/usma-class-of-1977-the-honor-scandal-and-beyond

[273] The West Point Center For Oral History. "USMA Class of 1977: The Honor Scandal and Beyond." Accessed August 30, 2023.
https://www.westpointcoh.org/interviews/usma-class-of-1977-the-honor-scandal-and-beyond

grounded in me a deep love of the country and a deep love of service to the country, I saw through that," he recalls.[274]

That environment, combined with hearing the stories of young men in his neighborhood returning from Vietnam, might have given a less-dedicated eighteen year-old pause when joining the army. Viola, however, was committed to the cause, and enrolled at West Point in the hopes of quickly making his way to Vietnam.

"I remember, in 1971, a young soldier from my neighborhood, whose family my family knew, got killed, and he was an infantryman," he recalls. "And I remember the impact it had on his family, especially his dad, who served so honorably in World War II. And I remember a real almost unquestioning allegiance to the idea that this was God's will, and fate had interceded in this man's adventure, the way it was meant to be, and he died an honorable death. And that stuck with me and sort of confirmed for me that the military was an honorable profession."[275]

With honor on his mind, Viola entered West Point in 1973. There, he met many like-minded individuals who were also dedicated to serving their country, though his class did eventually become embroiled in a widespread cheating scandal during his third year.[276] "My company was very unique, and I'm sure there were others like this – I don't have statistics on this – but we were what you called a sort of gray company. We were very, very Spartan and committed to the Academy and to its

---

[274] The West Point Center For Oral History. "USMA Class of 1977: The Honor Scandal and Beyond." Accessed August 30, 2023.
https://www.westpointcoh.org/interviews/usma-class-of-1977-the-honor-scandal-and-beyond

[275] The West Point Center For Oral History. "USMA Class of 1977: The Honor Scandal and Beyond." Accessed August 30, 2023.
https://www.westpointcoh.org/interviews/usma-class-of-1977-the-honor-scandal-and-beyond

[276] Times, James Feron Special to The New York. "More Than 90 Cadets at West Point Face Charges of Cheating on a Test." *The New York Times*, April 8, 1976, sec. Archives.
https://www.nytimes.com/1976/04/08/archives/more-than-90-cadets-at-west-point-face-charges-of-cheating-on-a.html.

principles. We were probably one of the most extraordinary in that regard," he remembers. "So my class and my company of A4 did not have one person's paper questioned, so we were almost in this kind of vacuum."

Here's what Viola had to say about the atmosphere of West Point and its effect on his peers during their time at the academy: "I think this place overwhelms you in a positive sense. If you are slightly potentialed to want to be here – slightly potentialed in your deepest personality to be selfless – if you have the United States of America as part of your core identity... you have to understand that the rewards of selfless leadership are enormously infectious. Dare I say they're definitional. So I don't want to paint the picture like we felt estranged here. The place was enormously proud of itself. We were enormously devout around the values and principles that we were living here. And dare I say even the cadets that suffered the current popular cultural gestalt of moral relativism while they were here, at their core desired and wanted to be combat leaders. You cannot help but that feeling."

After graduating from West Point in 1977, well after the end of the Vietnam War, Viola chose to serve as a platoon leader with the 101st Airborne Division at Fort Campbell, Kentucky. Moving down south was a tough decision for him given his family situation – during his Yearling, or sophomore, year, Viola's father fell ill and was forced to retire with just a small disability pension to support the family. Given his family's traditional values, his mother had focused all her life on keeping the home, meaning Viola had to work odd jobs during the summer to help out. His father's illness also made him the de facto head of the household, making the distance between Kentucky and Brooklyn even more difficult. "My classmates used to tease me," he recalls. "They said I had a very, very thick rubber band that was sewed in my back, and it would only stretch up to West Point and then spring back to my neighborhood in Brooklyn."[277]

---

[277] The West Point Center For Oral History. "USMA Class of 1977: The Honor Scandal and Beyond." Accessed August 30, 2023.

After serving for five years with the 101st Airborne, Viola made the tough decision to join the Army Reserves and leave Kentucky. His father had suffered a heart attack due to a congenital heart condition combined with his history of alcoholism, and his family needed him back home. "It was a pretty challenging situation," he said, "but here's the thing about the Army that's very hard to describe until you experience it. People, soldiers don't judge other soldiers. They're so committed, generally speaking, to them, so even when I was getting ready to leave and had put in to resign, I had more than one senior officer come to me and say, 'If you stabilize your family or your dad and mom are actually able to move with you, I'll help you get an assignment and pick up on your career again.' It was just amazing – you always feel as though you're part of the Army."

And so, he set off on his long (and eventually very successful) journey of entrepreneurship. But first, of course, came the growing pains that accompany leaving the structured career path of the military for the civilian workforce. "I had absolutely no idea – I never really took serious in my own contemplation the idea that I would ever leave the Army," he remembers, "so I didn't know how to look for a job. I applied – I paid someone to write a resume. I wrote a clumsy letter and sent it out to companies that I looked up at the library – back in those days, that's what you did. And I got absolutely no responses, and it was a pretty tough period – it was still a deep recession." Eventually, though, things started looking up. By August of 1982, he'd found a job working as a runner for brokers on Wall Street, and was taking night classes (only because his mother told him to) at New York City Law School for his J.D., which he would receive in June of 1983.[278]

Soon after earning his J.D., Viola started working on the trading floor of the New York Mercantile Exchange (NYMEX),

---

https://www.westpointcoh.org/interviews/usma-class-of-1977-the-honor-scandal-and-beyond

[278] New York Law School. "1983 Commencement Program," June 1983. https://digitalcommons.nyls.edu/cgi/viewcontent.cgi?article=1023&context=commencement_progs.

gathering $10,000 from his Army pay, friends, and family to purchase a seat as a "local" trader on the exchange.[279] "My friends said, 'You have to come down here. You were always very good at mathematics,'" he remembers. "And from the first day I entered the trading floor, I couldn't believe it, because it had many of the physical characteristics of being around a platoon environment."[280]

"My management leadership operation, dare I say, capacity, capability, is bounded in the skills around platoon leadership. If you believe that you cannot effectively, comprehensively, lead more than four persons other than yourself on a physical day-to-day level, then everything you ever wanted to know about anything, you've learned in platoon leadership."

Using his analytical mind and leadership skills, Viola quickly climbed the corporate ladder, gaining a reputation as an aggressive and successful trader specializing in gasoline markets. Former NYMEX chairman Lou Guttman said that as a young trader, Viola "exuded leadership. His personality was amazing. He drew people in. He was a phenomenal speaker. Even if he didn't know what he was talking about, he sounded like he knew what he was saying. He was an astute businessman and an extreme opportunist."[281]

He made millions trading oil before and after the first Gulf War, gaining new bullet points on his resume as his bank accounts continued to grow. His positions at NYMEX include

---

[279] Osipovich, Alexander, Damian Paletta, and Bradley Hope. "Donald Trump Selects Trading Firm Founder Vincent Viola as Army Secretary." *Wall Street Journal*, December 19, 2016, sec. US.
http://www.wsj.com/articles/donald-trump-selects-trading-firm-founder-vincent-viola-as-army-secretary-1482159528.

[280] The West Point Center For Oral History. "USMA Class of 1977: The Honor Scandal and Beyond." Accessed August 30, 2023.
https://www.westpointcoh.org/interviews/usma-class-of-1977-the-honor-scandal-and-beyond

[281] "New York Businessman Leading Group Purchasing Florida Panthers | Miami Herald." Accessed August 30, 2023.
https://www.miamiherald.com/sports/nhl/florida-panthers/article1955201.html.

serving on the Board of Directors, as chairman of the Technology Committee, the Natural Gas Advisory Committee, and the Facilities Committee, and as co-chairman of the Options Committee, Vice Chairman of NYMEX from 1993 to 1996 before eventually becoming chairman of the exchange in 2001.[282]

He was able to successfully steer the exchange through the post-9/11 world. Following the attacks, he helped colleagues escape Manhattan while also going as far as airlifting generators to the NYMEX building so that trading could continue within a week of the attacks.[283] At the same time, he stayed true to his patriotic nature, donating $2 million to create the Counter-Terrorism Center at West Point. According to a statement by NYMEX's board, his "heroic leadership served as a beacon to thousands of Exchange members and staff, providing us with the fortitude to resume operations and preserve the efficiency of the American economy and global energy and metals markets in the face of this great tragedy…His wholehearted determination, refusal to be thwarted, and skilled comportment with public officials were the impetus behind the Exchange being the only business west of Ground Zero to open on September 17 and for several months thereafter – preserving the livelihoods of tens of thousands of individuals and families in New York and worldwide. His actions embody the American Spirit in its most noble form."[284]

While this would be quite the successful career for any businessman, Viola had his sights set on even more. In 2002, Viola and a few business partners started two electric trading

---

[282] The National Italian American Foundation. "Vincent Viola." Accessed August 31, 2023. https://www.niaf.org/wallofhonor/vincent-viola/.
[283] Lamothe, Dan. "Army Veteran Vincent Viola, Billionaire Owner of the Florida Panthers, Named Trump's Army Secretary." *Washington Post*, October 27, 2021. https://www.washingtonpost.com/news/checkpoint/wp/2016/12/19/army-veteran-vincent-viola-billionaire-owner-of-the-florida-panthers-named-trumps-army-secretary/.
[284] NHL.com. "Vincent Viola Becomes Owner Of The Florida Panthers." Accessed August 31, 2023. https://www.nhl.com/panthers/news/vincent-viola-becomes-owner-of-the-florida-panthers/c-684466.

firms, using the electronic trading techniques developed by the companies to further his fortune as a forerunner of modern market makers. In 2008, he merged the two companies to form Virtu Financial, the company which catapulted him into becoming one of the richest men in America. Virtu specializes in market-making, essentially using algorithms to spot small opportunities for profits in flipping securities. "He took the market-making skills he learned on the Nymex floor and automated them," said a close friend of Viola regarding Virtu's business model.[285]

In 2013, Viola and Doug Cifu, the Chief Executive of Virtu, pooled their money to purchase the NHL's flailing Florida Panthers. After an adjustment period, his focus on analytics and "moneyball" led to the Panthers becoming postseason regulars, making it to the playoffs four years in a row after decades of struggles prior to the purchase.

In 2015, Viola took Virtu public. As of August 2023, the company had a market capitalization of over $3 billion, with Viola's own net worth hovering around that same number. In 2016, President Donald Trump named Viola as his pick for secretary of the Army, though the plan fell through because he was unable to comply with Pentagon regulations regarding his business positions. He and his family still live in New York City to this day, and he's still involved in multiple ventures. He's a member of the Chairman's Council for the NBA's Brooklyn Nets, involved in many top-level decisions for the organization, and is also part-owner of the St. Elias Stables, which produced Always Dreaming, 2017's Kentucky Derby Winner. He's still also actively involved in his many companies and philanthropic ventures.

---

[285] Osipovich, Alexander, Damian Paletta, and Bradley Hope. "Donald Trump Selects Trading Firm Founder Vincent Viola as Army Secretary." *Wall Street Journal*, December 19, 2016, sec. US.
http://www.wsj.com/articles/donald-trump-selects-trading-firm-founder-vincent-viola-as-army-secretary-1482159528.

VIII.

Sam Walton

U.S. Army

Walmart

While it's currently the world's biggest private employer and largest business by revenue, Walmart began as a small series of five-and-dime stores located in the Ozarks. The innovation and leadership needed to scale the business from a single discount store to the retail giant it's become today can largely be credited to one man: a limited-duty military veteran from the middle of nowhere with a passion for retail.

That man, Samuel Moore Walton, was born in 1918 in the small town of Kingfisher, Oklahoma to Thomas Gibson Walton and Nancy Lee. He describes his father Thomas as both "an awfully hard worker" and "a bit of a character."[286] The older Walton woke up early and worked long hours, but also enjoyed bartering for just about anything – at one point, Sam Walton recalls, Thomas traded his watch for a hog, which the Waltons had for dinner that same night. While he liked to wheel and deal like no other, Thomas didn't have the entrepreneurial drive to start his own business, instead working many different odd jobs to provide more for his family. Sam's mother Nancy, though, did have a bit of that drive – she ran a small milk-selling side business to help keep the family afloat.

Growing up during the Great Depression set a certain tone for the Waltons, which you might be able to figure out from the previous anecdotes about the family's hustle – every member of the family was expected to pitch in. "I started selling magazine subscriptions, probably as young as seven or eight years old," he recalls, "and I had paper routes from the seventh grade all through college. I raised and sold rabbits and pigeons too, nothing really unusual for country boys at the time. I learned from a very young age that it was important for us kids to help provide for the home, to be contributors rather than just takers. In the process, of course, we learned how much hard work it took to get your hands on a dollar, and that when you did it was worth something. One thing my mother and dad shared completely was

---

[286] Walton, Sam, and John Huey. Sam Walton: Made In America. Reissue edition. New York: Bantam, 1993.

their approach to money: they just didn't spend it."[287] Even after he made his billions, Walton held his parents' lesson close, becoming notorious for things like driving old trucks with two missing hubcaps and working out of an office cubicle furnished with "early Holiday Inn" decor.[288]

"I don't know what causes a person to be ambitious, but it is a fact that I have been overblessed with drive and ambition from the time I hit the ground," writes Walton. "Our mother was extremely ambitious for her kids. She read a lot and loved education, although she didn't have too much herself ... Mother must have been a pretty special motivator, because I took her seriously when she told me I should always try to be the best I could at whatever I took on. So, I have always pursued everything I was interested in with a true passion – some would say obsession – to win."[289]

This drive was evident in Walton as early as the eighth grade, when he became the youngest Eagle Scout ever in the state of Missouri. In high school, he became class president, worked hard to get on the honor roll, and was voted "Most Versatile Boy" – in addition to being a starting point guard for the school's state champion basketball team, and the first-string quarterback for the school's state champion football team.

After graduation, Walton headed to college as an ROTC cadet in order to further his prospects. Similarly to high school, he found success in almost every area of college life – he was accepted to the University of Missouri chapter of Beta Theta Phi, the top scholastic fraternity at the time. Soon, he set his sights on becoming a leader in the student body, and began applying for every student leadership position he could. "I learned early on that one of the secrets to campus leadership was the simplest thing of all: speak to people coming down the sidewalk before

---

[287] Walton, Sam, and John Huey. Sam Walton: Made In America. Reissue edition. New York: Bantam, 1993.
[288] Chicago Tribune. "The Frugal Lifestyle of the King of Thrift," December 17, 1990. https://archive.ph/5ZGhv.
[289] Walton, Sam, and John Huey. Sam Walton: Made In America. Reissue edition. New York: Bantam, 1993.

they speak to you," he recalls. "Before long, I probably knew more students than anybody in the university, and they recognized me and considered me their friend."[290] He parlayed this popularity into a variety of elected offices, becoming a rush captain for the Betas, president of the senior men's honor society, president of the senior class, and captain and president of the Scabbard and Blade, the ROTC's top honor society.

All this time, Walton was also paying his own way through school thanks to the lasting effects of the Great Depression. "We hired Sam to deliver newspapers, and he really became our chief salesman," said his former boss. "When school started, we had a drive to get the kids in the fraternities and sororities to subscribe. And Sam was the boy we had do that because he could sell more than anybody else. He was good. He was really good. And dedicated. And he did a lot of other things besides deliver newspapers. In fact, he was a little scatterbrained at times. He'd have so many things going, he'd almost forget one. But boy, when he focused on something, that was it."[291] Besides helping out the paper business, Walton also had a few other side jobs, including waiting tables in exchange for meals and a position as a head lifeguard at a swimming pool. In total, his gigs were earning him around $5,000 annually – a good sum for the time.

He graduated from the University of Missouri in June of 1940 with a business degree, intending to head to the University of Pennsylvania's Wharton School of Finance. Unfortunately, he realized that he wouldn't be able to afford tuition even with all his odd jobs, and instead took up a recruitment offer at a JC Penney in Des Moines, Iowa – thus beginning his long journey into the world of retail. "Maybe I was born to be a merchant, maybe it was fate," he writes looking back at the decision. "I don't know about that kind of stuff. But I know this for sure: I loved retail from the very beginning, and I still love it today. Not

---

[290] Walton, Sam, and John Huey. Sam Walton: Made In America. Reissue edition. New York: Bantam, 1993.
[291] Walton, Sam, and John Huey. Sam Walton: Made In America. Reissue edition. New York: Bantam, 1993.

that it went smooth right off the bat." He worked at the JC Penney in Des Moines for about eighteen months, learning more about the retail industry, before the Army called his name.

In early 1942, as a hot-blooded young man looking to head to the front in the wake of Pearl Harbor, Walton took a physical for combat duty with the Army. Unfortunately for his heroic aspirations, the Army discovered that he had a minor heart irregularity, barring him from any combat roles. In a funk from the rejection, Walton still left behind his retail job (figuring that the Army would call him up for limited duty sometime soon), heading to Tulsa to see what the oil industry was like. In Tulsa, he met his future wife, Helen Robson. "She was pretty and smart and educated, ambitious and opinionated and strong-willed – with ideas and plans of her own," he reminisces. "Also, like me, she was an athlete who loved the outdoors, and she had lots of energy."[292]

Soon after meeting Helen, he was called for active duty by the Army. By this time, he felt a little better about his direction in life, he recalls: "By the time I went into the Army, I had two things settled: I knew who I wanted to marry, and I knew what I wanted to do for a living – retailing." With those goals in mind, he accepted his ROTC commission as a second lieutenant in the U.S. Army Intelligence Corps. "I wish I could recount a valiant military career – like my brother Bud, who was a Navy bomber pilot on a carrier in the Pacific – but my service stint was really fairly ordinary time spent as a lieutenant and then as a captain doing things like supervising security at aircraft plants and POW camps in California and around the country," he said of his military service.[293]

Leaving service in 1945, Walton was filled with a sense of purpose, and quickly set off into the world of retail. Pooling $5,000 of his own money with a $20,000 loan from Helen's father, he became owner of a Ben Franklin variety store in

---

[292] Walton, Sam, and John Huey. Sam Walton: Made In America. Reissue edition. New York: Bantam, 1993.
[293] Walton, Sam, and John Huey. Sam Walton: Made In America. Reissue edition. New York: Bantam, 1993.

Newport, Arkansas, part of a chain of the five-and-dime stores across the south. As a new business owner, he learned a lot about how (and how not) to run a retail business from Butler Brothers, the company which owned the whole Ben Franklin franchising operation.

While the company expected their franchisees to operate strictly by the book, Walton soon began looking for ways to squeeze more of a profit from his single store, which was struggling to stay afloat with low sales, high rent, and the strong competition put up by another five-and-dime across the street. He began reaching out to manufacturers directly in order to circumvent the fees associated with being a franchisee, lowering his prices, and running his own promotional deals to get more people in his store – a concept now known as discount marketing.

"Here's the simple lesson we learned," he recalls of that first store. "By cutting your price, you can boost your sales to a point where you earn far more at the cheaper retail price than you would have by selling the item at the higher price. In retailer language, you can lower your markup but earn more because of the increased volume."[294] The store quickly became a top performer in the region for the Ben Franklin chain thanks to his constant tweaking and negotiation, and Walton set his sights on expansion.

He bought up another property in Newport, setting up a department store with the help of his brother Bud, who'd come back from his time in the Navy. Bud helped Sam run both the five-and-dime and the department store, and remembers that first Ben Franklin as the first Walmart, in spirit at least. "That Newport store was really the beginning of where Wal-Mart is today," he recalls. " We did everything. We would wash windows, sweep floors, trim windows ... everything it took to run a store. We had to keep expenses to a minimum. That is where it started, years ago. Our money was made by controlling expenses. That,

---

[294] Walton, Sam, and John Huey. Sam Walton: Made In America. Reissue edition. New York: Bantam, 1993.

and Sam always being ingenious. He never stopped trying to do something different."[295]

Eventually, though, the good things he had going in Newport came to an end. Walton had signed a five-year lease for that first Ben Franklin store; at the end of that lease, it was the top-performing franchise in its whole six-state region, earning over $250,000 in sales with $40,000 in profit. For all his evident retail genius, though, Walton somehow forgot to renew the lease for the building, and his landlord declined to help him out – instead, he offered to purchase the business, inventory and all. With no way out, Walton let go of both of his Newport stores and moved on to a different town.

By May of 1950, the Waltons ended up in Bentonville, Arkansas, a sleepy town of just 3,000 people . There, with the help of his father-in-law, he bought out another struggling variety store, turning it into another Ben Franklin franchise (though he named it Walton's Five-and-Dime). That new store was where Walton's innovation hit a new stride. At the time, most variety stores didn't allow customers to roam aisles of merchandise – instead, clerks would bring the goods to the customer at the counter. With Walton's Five-and-Dime, though, Walton tested out the first-ever self-service store in Arkansas (and the third in America) to a resounding success. Soon after that store was up and running, he also looked to diversify his portfolio, setting up another Ben Franklin store in another small town 25 miles south of Bentonville in 1952, which raked in $90,000 in sales in its very first year.

With two businesses now up and running, Walton continued opening up Ben Franklin franchises nearby, ending up with a store in Tennessee and another in Missouri. Those franchises took off quickly as well, until a literal disaster struck – a tornado had hit one of his best performing stores, located in Ruskin Heights, Missouri, and leveled the whole place. It took Walton quite the drive to get there, and that incident, combined

---

[295] Walton, Sam, and John Huey. Sam Walton: Made In America. Reissue edition. New York: Bantam, 1993.

with the hours he was already spending on driving back and forth between his stores convinced him to learn to fly a plane.

"One day I got a call from Sam," recalls his brother Bud, "and he said, 'Meet me in Kansas City, I want to buy an airplane.' Boy, it took me by such surprise. I always thought he was the world's worst driver and even my father wouldn't ever let Sam drive him. I thought, 'He will kill himself the first year.' So I did everything in the world to try and talk him out of that first airplane ... But then we were putting some more stores in around Little Rock, and one day he says, 'Let's go to Little Rock.' I hadn't flown since the Navy in the Pacific, and I was always used to water. Here we were with Sam at the stick going over all these trees and mountains. It was the longest trip I ever took. That was the start of the Wal-Mart aviation era."[296]

"We never could have maintained the operating controls of communications without having the ability to get into our stores on a consistent basis," said Sam Walton himself.[297]

After he took to the air, Walton soon began opening up new franchises at a record pace. He had, as he puts it, "store fever." By 1960, he owned a total of fifteen stores raking in $1.4 million in sales overall. Walton had become the largest independent variety store operator in the country, but he felt that "the business itself seemed a little limited."[298] As discount variety stores like Kmart began to spring up around the U.S., the Ben Franklin franchising fees were taking their toll on Walton's earnings.

In 1962, Walton opened his first-ever real Wal-Mart in the town of Rogers, Arkansas. The store differed from his usual five-and-dime Ben Franklin franchises in its pure focus on discounting – it was closer to a giant warehouse full of cheap

---

[296] Walton, Sam, and John Huey. Sam Walton: Made In America. Reissue edition. New York: Bantam, 1993.
[297] "Walton, Samuel Moore - Encyclopedia of Arkansas." Accessed September 8, 2023. https://encyclopediaofarkansas.net/entries/samuel-moore-walton-1792/
[298] Walton, Sam, and John Huey. Sam Walton: Made In America. Reissue edition. New York: Bantam, 1993.

merchandise than the small-town corner stores he was used to running. He'd subconsciously learned the basics of discount marketing from his earlier retail ventures, but he spent some time flying around the country, visiting various discount retailers, and learning some lessons. One discount store owner said it best: "Buy it low, stack it high, sell it cheap." The key here was volume – the most successful discount stores at the time were raking in about $2 million in annual sales per store, thanks to the sheer volume of goods they stocked and sold. Walton and Helen put up 95% of the capital used to start the store, as most people he asked to pitch in didn't believe in the concept.

The first Wal-Mart did good numbers, pulling in over a million dollars in sales, compared to the $200,000 to $300,000 a normal Ben Franklin did annually. That was enough to convince Walton of the concept, and he quickly opened two new Wal-Marts in Springdale, Arkansas (a bigger town than Rogers) and Harrison (a smaller town than Rogers).

"The store was only 12,000 square feet," he recalls of that second Wal-Mart, "and had an 8-foot ceiling and a concrete floor, with bare-boned wooden plank fixtures ... Ours was just barely put together – highly promotional, truly ugly, heavy with merchandise – but for 20 percent less than the competition. We were trying to find out if customers in a town of 6,000 people would come to our barn and buy the same merchandise strictly because of price. The answer was yes. We found out they did, and they wanted it."[299]

The two newer stores also took off, which was when he knew "in his bones" that the concept would work. By the late 1960's, he'd set up a dozen Wal-Marts around Arkansas. Those early stores had almost no logistical systems in place, and their interiors were even less organized than their systems. "Everything was just piled up on tables, with no rhyme or reason whatsoever," Walton remembers. He eventually came up with the idea of storing merchandise in categories or departments,

---

[299] Walton, Sam, and John Huey. Sam Walton: Made In America. Reissue edition. New York: Bantam, 1993.

and also slowly established things like a basic inventory system, replenishment systems, and a distribution system.

In order to build out Wal-Mart's systems, Walton was an early adopter of computerization, attending classes on how to use an IBM computer in a retail business as early as the mid-1960's. One speaker at those classes was Abe Marks, a member of the National Mass Retailers' institution who would turn out to be a close business associate of Walton's over the next decade.

"What we really helped [Walton] with in the early days was really logistics," said Marks. "It's like in the Army. You can move troops all over the world, but unless you have the capacity to supply them with ammunition and food, there's no sense putting them out there. Sam understood that. He knew that he was already in what the trade calls an 'absentee ownership' situation. That just means you're puting out stores where you, as management, aren't. If the wanted to grow he had to learn to control it. So to service these stores you've got to have timely information: How much merchandise is in the store? What is it? What's selling and what's not? What is to be ordered, marked down, replaced? ... Anyway, the man's a genius. He realized – even at the rudimentary level he was on in 1996, operating those few stores that he had – that he couldn't expand beyond that horizon unless he had the ability to capture this information on paper so that he could control his operations, no matter where he might be. He became, really, the best utilizer of information to control absentee ownerships that there's ever been. Which gave him the ability to open as many stores as he opens, and run them as well as he runs them, and to be as profitable as he makes them."[300] Walton had figured out, a decade before computers would become meaningful tools, that he would need the future technology to grow and scale his business.

By 1970, Walton had opened eighteen Wal-Marts, cobbled together by tight communication, hands-on management, and a growing logistical network. Walton had also

---

[300] Walton, Sam, and John Huey. Sam Walton: Made In America. Reissue edition. New York: Bantam, 1993.

purchased a small bank along the way, gained capital from different investors, and felt that the Wal-Mart concept was ready to move on to the next level. After some restructuring and discussion, Wal-Mart became a publicly traded company on October 1, 1970, offering 300,000 shares at $15 apiece. That first day, around 800 people and organizations became Wal-Mart shareholders, mainly people Walton knew personally or had partnered with in the past. Those first shareholders, according to Walton himself, "made an absolute killing."

Helen was against going public soon after it happened – she didn't like the public-facing part of the business, dealing with questions from stockholders and making the Walton family's business, well, public. "Helen's right, of course, about the downside of taking the company public," said Walton. "It did end up bringing us a lot of unwanted attention. But coming back from New York that day, I experienced one of the greatest feelings of my life, knowing that all our debts were paid off. The Walton family only owned 61 percent of Wal-Mart after that day, but we were able to pay off all those bankers, and from that day on, we haven't borrowed one dime personally to support Wal-Mart. The company has rolled along on its own and financed itself. Going public really turned the company loose to grow, and it took a huge load off me."[301]

Over the next decade, Wal-Mart would take off on a trajectory that even Walton himself couldn't believe. By 1974, there were 78 Wal-Marts operating in the eight states, bringing in $168 million in sales. By 1976, that number would balloon to 125 stores with $340 million in sales, and by 1980 – just one decade after the IPO, the brand was operating a whopping 276 stores with $1.2 billion in sales.[302]

The sustained growth over a decade was supported both by Wal-Mart's dogged focus on delivering the highest discounts possible to its customers, as well as its logistics systems, which

---

[301] Walton, Sam, and John Huey. Sam Walton: Made In America. Reissue edition. New York: Bantam, 1993.
[302] Walton, Sam, and John Huey. Sam Walton: Made In America. Reissue edition. New York: Bantam, 1993.

made sure the company was able to expand its capabilities without bloat. One of Wal-Mart's biggest logistical strengths during this period was its warehouse network, which allowed the company to quickly establish new stores in remote, rural areas while keeping them within its distribution range. The warehouses were the beating heart of its massive growth, making high-volume purchases at lower prices while allowing the company to distribute goods optimally with its in-house trucking services.[303]

Another key development in keeping Wal-Mart's vast network of stores and employees bought in was the company's profit-sharing plan. The plan offers all Wal-Mart associates who've worked with the company for at least a year for over 1,000 hours per year the opportunity to invest a portion of their pay into Wal-Mart stock, both letting them build their investment portfolio while also making them more personally invested in their workplace's success.

By 1987, there were 1,198 Wal-Mart stores operating nationwide, making $15.9 billion in sales and employing over 200,000 associates.[304] That same year, the company completed its $24 million investment in a private satellite communications system (again showcasing Walton's willingness to adapt to the times), allowing two-way voice and data transmissions between stores, as well as one-way video transmissions out of the company's headquarters in Bentonville, Arkansas.[305] That system, the world's biggest private satellite network at the time, allowed the nerve center in Bentonvillle to monitor inventory and sales while communicating instantaneously with its stores,

---

[303] "Sam Walton | Biography & Facts | Britannica," August 11, 2023. https://www.britannica.com/biography/Sam-Walton.
[304] "Wal-Mart Facts - Get the Facts and Latest News about Wal-Mart from Wal-Mart.," July 19, 2006.
https://web.archive.org/web/20060719071543/http://www.walmartfacts.com/content/default.aspx?id=3.
[305] "The Hindu Business Line : Satellite Adds Speed to Wal-Mart," September 27, 2007.
https://web.archive.org/web/20070927012640/http://www.blonnet.com/2005/07/17/stories/2005071700141600.htm.

making the business even more agile and responsive than ever before. "Instead of the retailer pushing products into the system, customers 'pull' products when and where they need them," observed a 1992 analysis of Wal-Mart's systems. "The job of senior management at Wal-Mart, then, is not to tell individual store managers what to do but to create an environment where they can learn from the market -- and from each other."[306]

In 1988, Walton stepped down from his post as Wal-Mart's CEO (though he of course kept one foot in the door as the company' chairman). Two years later, Wal-Mart passed Sears, Roebuck & Company to become the largest retailer in America, and also operated two locations in Mexico. That same year, Walton was diagnosed with multiple myeloma, a bone cancer. In 1992, he passed away from the disease, just one month after receiving the Presidential Medal of Freedom, which hailed him as an "American original" who "embodies the entrepreneurial spirit and epitomizes the American dream."[307] At that time, there were 1,735 Wal-Marts operating globally, with 380,000 employees and annual sales of almost $50 billion.[308]

Here are the (shortened) "Sam's Rules for Building a Business," written by the man himself in an autobiography he worked on up until his passing:

1. COMMIT to your business. Believe in it more than anybody else.
2. SHARE your profits with all your associates, and treat them as partners. In turn, they will treat you as a

---

[306] Hayes, Thomas C. "Sam Walton Is Dead At 74; the Founder Of Wal-Mart Stores." *The New York Times*, April 6, 1992, sec. U.S. https://www.nytimes.com/1992/04/06/us/sam-walton-is-dead-at-74-the-founder-of-wal-mart-stores.html.
[307] Hayes, Thomas C. "Sam Walton Is Dead At 74; the Founder Of Wal-Mart Stores." *The New York Times*, April 6, 1992, sec. U.S. https://www.nytimes.com/1992/04/06/us/sam-walton-is-dead-at-74-the-founder-of-wal-mart-stores.html.
[308] "Sam Walton | Biography & Facts | Britannica," August 11, 2023. https://www.britannica.com/biography/Sam-Walton.

partner, and together you will all perform beyond your wildest expectations.
3. MOTIVATE your partners. Money and ownership alone aren't enough ... Set high goals, encourage competition, and then keep score.
4. COMMUNICATE everything you possibly can to your partners. The more they know, the more they'll understand. The more they understand, the more they'll care. Once they care, there's no stopping them.
5. APPRECIATE everything your associates do for the business. A paycheck and a stock option will buy one kind of loyalty. But all of us like to be told how much somebody appreciates what we do for them.
6. CELEBRATE your successes. Find some humor in your failures. Don't take yourself too seriously.
7. LISTEN to everyone in your company. And figure out ways to get them talking. The folks on the front lines – the ones who actually talk to the customer – are the only ones who really know what's going on out there.
8. EXCEED your customers' expectations. If you do, they'll come back over and over.
9. CONTROL your expenses better than your competition. This is where you can always find the competitive advantage.
10. SWIM upstream. Go the other way. If everybody else is doing it one way, there's a good chance you can find your niche by going in exactly the opposite direction.

"Those are some pretty ordinary rules, some would even say simplistic," he adds. "The hard part, the real challenge, is to constantly figure out ways to execute them. You can't just keep doing what works one time, because everything around you is always changing to succeed, you have to stay in front of that change."[309]

---

[309] Walton, Sam, and John Huey. Sam Walton: Made In America. Reissue edition. New York: Bantam, 1993.

X.

Jim Kimsey

U.S. Army

AOL

Jim Kimsey, co-founder of AOL, was born James Verlin Kimsey on Sept. 15, 1939, in Washington, D.C.[310] He spent most of his young life in Arlington, Virginia, where his family struggled to make ends meet. Kimsey, the eldest of five children, remembers, "I grew up in a fairly tough environment. My youngest brother was autistic, and my parents had a rough time dealing with the problems that went along with his condition."[311] His father, a veteran of World War 1, kept the family scraping by financially with his low-level position at the federal government, and Kimsey had to start work early on to support the family. He worked a paper route from a young age before swapping to caddying once he was strong enough to lug around a bag of golf clubs.[312] Despite the hardships his family faced through his childhood, Kimsey still kept a positive attitude for his future, instilled in him by his mother. "I had the idea early on that I could be anything I wanted to be," he remembers. "That's one of the great things about this country. The message permeates the atmosphere: Every kid born in America can grow up to be president. I believed that."[313]

Kimsey channeled this energy into his education: early on in his student life, he earned the nickname "Lightbulb" for his academic skill.[314] With his mother's help, Kimsey earned a scholarship at Gonzaga College High School in Washington, D.C., making him one of just four scholarship recipients in his class. To get to school every day, Kimsey had to commute across the Potomac River, meaning he had to either pay the fare for a

---

[310] Protess, Ben. "Jim Kimsey Dies at 76; AOL Co-Founder Influenced Generation of Net Providers." *The New York Times*, March 2, 2016, sec. Technology. https://www.nytimes.com/2016/03/03/technology/jim-kimsey-dies-at-76-aol-co-founder-influenced-generation-of-net-providers.html.
[311] "James V. Kimsey." Accessed May 23, 2022. https://horatioalger.org/members/.
[312] "James V. Kimsey." Accessed May 23, 2022. https://horatioalger.org/members/.
[313] "James V. Kimsey." Accessed May 23, 2022. https://horatioalger.org/members/.
[314] "James V. Kimsey." Accessed May 23, 2022. https://horatioalger.org/members/.

streetcar or hitchhike his way to the classroom. He often resorted to the second option to save money. At school, Kimsey dealt with some discipline issues despite his natural gifts, leading to him getting kicked out of Gonzaga College High in his senior year for being, in his own words, "unruly and obstreperous."[315] His mother promptly went to St. John's College High School in Washington, D.C. and begged for the chance for her son to take a scholarship test, which Kimsey passed, allowing him to finish out his high school education.

After wrapping up at St. John's, Kimsey earned yet another scholarship at Georgetown University, which he attended for a year. As a freshman, Kimsey was inspired by military media like The Long Gray Line and The West Point Story, as well as his father's service, and felt an urge to serve his country – with the added bonus that being able to wear a uniform might help his chances with getting dates. With the help of his mother's sister, Kimsey took an aptitude test held by Senator Murray from Montana, who gave him an appointment to West Point after he earned the highest score of all the candidates who took the test.[316] Despite earning his place at West Point, many around Kimsey doubted his ability to succeed at the school: "So many people were convinced that I wouldn't graduate from West Point that I was motivated, though I was not a very good cadet, to stay and graduate, which I did," he remembers.[317]

During his time at the academy, Kimsey learned key life lessons in honor, duty, and, most importantly, accountability, helping him grow out of his youthful unruliness: "They told me there are three answers to every question: 'Yes, sir,' 'No, sir,' 'No excuse, sir.' Later, when I was in combat, those words came back

---

[315] "Interview with James Verlin Kimsey." Accessed May 26, 2022. https://memory.loc.gov/diglib/vhp-stories/loc.natlib.afc2001001.84178/mv0001001.stream?start=4.
[316] "Interview with James Verlin Kimsey." Accessed May 26, 2022. https://memory.loc.gov/diglib/vhp-stories/loc.natlib.afc2001001.84178/mv0001001.stream?start=4.
[317] "Interview with James Verlin Kimsey." Accessed May 26, 2022. https://memory.loc.gov/diglib/vhp-stories/loc.natlib.afc2001001.84178/mv0001001.stream?start=4.

to me, and I realized that there is no defense for failure. It was a valuable lesson that taught me never to settle for less than optimal results in anything I undertook," he recalled.[318] Kimsey graduated with the class of 1962, with a degree in military engineering. He earned a Distinguished Graduate Award, and was "overwhelmed with the delicious irony of being in the company of people like MacArthur and Eisenhower and other notable people."[319]

Following his graduation, Kimsey reluctantly followed through with his four-year commitment to serve post-graduation. He applied to become an Airborne Ranger, hoping that he would be denied and would not have to serve, but to his surprise he was allowed to attend Ranger School. Luckily, Kimsey found that, unlike his classmates, he enjoyed Ranger School, and he joined the 82nd Airborne Division as a company commander.[320] With the 82nd Airborne, his first deployment was the U.S. invasion of the Dominican Republic, commanding one of the first U.S. companies on the ground in 1965. There, he helped push rebel commander Francisco Caamaño out of Santo Domingo before heading back to the U.S.[321,322]

Soon after his short stint in the Caribbean, Kimsey set out on his first tour in Vietnam. He'd requested the tour because he expected the war to finish quickly and wanted to participate in

---

[318] "James V. Kimsey." Accessed May 23, 2022. https://horatioalger.org/members/.
[319] "Interview with James Verlin Kimsey." Accessed May 26, 2022. https://memory.loc.gov/diglib/vhp-stories/loc.natlib.afc2001001.84178/mv0001001.stream?start=4.
[320] "West Point Association of Graduates." Accessed May 23, 2022. https://www.westpointaog.org/page.aspx?pid=2714.
[321] Zipkin, Nina. "AOL Co-Founder Jim Kimsey Dies at 76." Connecticut Post, March 3, 2016. https://www.ctpost.com/news/article/AOL-Co-founder-Jim-Kimsey-Dies-at-76-6868064.php.
[322] "Interview with James Verlin Kimsey." Accessed May 26, 2022. https://memory.loc.gov/diglib/vhp-stories/loc.natlib.afc2001001.84178/mv0001001.stream?start=4

fighting communism.[323] In Vietnam, he was assigned to work as an assistant in a "quiet area" of Quang Ngai province in South Vietnam.[324] Soon after his deployment, he was called to lead a 12-man District Advisory Team at Duc Pho, a district of Quang Ngai, after U.S. forces were overrun in the area.[325,326,327] In Duc Pho, he "never had a day go by when someone didn't shoot at [him] for one reason or another."[328] In addition to normal service, Kimsey helped found an orphanage for war orphans, finishing the efforts of his predecessors at Duc Pho. They had raised funds for the orphanage before being overrun, but higher-ups wanted the orphanage to be built in Saigon. As the story gained press back in the U.S., Kimsey kept pushing for the orphanage to stay in Duc Pho because he knew just how many war orphans the U.S. had created in the area.[329] Kimsey also knew that, with a newsworthy orphanage being built in his area, more troops would be sent to his command to protect the U.S.'s new asset. The troops were badly needed as U.S. forces were spread thin at the time, and all Kimsey had to command was a "ragtag" group of men.[330] With enough cajoling, leadership was

---

[323] "Interview with James Verlin Kimsey." Accessed May 26, 2022. https://memory.loc.gov/diglib/vhp-stories/loc.natlib.afc2001001.84178/mv0001001.stream?start=4.

[324] "Interview with James Verlin Kimsey." Accessed May 26, 2022. https://memory.loc.gov/diglib/vhp-stories/loc.natlib.afc2001001.84178/mv0001001.stream?start=4.

[325] "James V. Kimsey." Accessed May 23, 2022. https://horatioalger.org/members/.

[326] "West Point Association of Graduates." Accessed May 23, 2022. https://www.westpointaog.org/page.aspx?pid=2714.

[327] "Interview with James Verlin Kimsey." Accessed May 26, 2022. https://memory.loc.gov/diglib/vhp-stories/loc.natlib.afc2001001.84178/mv0001001.stream?start=4.

[328] "Interview with James Verlin Kimsey." Accessed May 26, 2022. https://memory.loc.gov/diglib/vhp-stories/loc.natlib.afc2001001.84178/mv0001001.stream?start=4.

[329] "Interview with James Verlin Kimsey." Accessed May 26, 2022. https://memory.loc.gov/diglib/vhp-stories/loc.natlib.afc2001001.84178/mv0001001.stream?start=4.

[330] "Interview with James Verlin Kimsey." Accessed May 26, 2022. https://memory.loc.gov/diglib/vhp-stories/loc.natlib.afc2001001.84178/mv0001001.stream?start=4.

convinced to place the orphanage in Duc Pho, so (using his West Point training) Kimsey set about writing up plans for the project. The orphanage was built with the help of local Vietnamese labor and a trio of nuns were brought to Duc Pho to staff the place. Instead of taking a six-month staffing job (in Vietnam, officers served six months in the field and six months away from the front lines), Kimsey chose to stay in Duc Pho to ensure the orphanage got up and running smoothly. The orphanage still survives to this day, though it moved to Qui Nhon once the Northern Vietnamese overran its home region.

After finishing his first tour of Vietnam, Kimsey was assigned to Fort Lewis near Tacoma, Washington, for 18 months. He remembers his stay in the Evergreen State fondly, calling it the "most pleasant time I had in the Army."[331] At Fort Lewis, he raised his young family with his ex-wife in a house on a lake, where he often took his two young sons fishing. His time at the base coincided with a rise in anti-war sentiment in the U.S., and that, combined with his new family, made Kimsey less enthusiastic to embark on his second tour of Vietnam.

Despite his apprehensions, he left for Vietnam a second time in 1968, heading to Saigon first. There, he was recruited by a higher-up named Ace Ellis, who brought him to work on the Phoenix Program under former Director of Central Intelligence William Colby.[332] The Phoenix Program was a U.S. counterintelligence program which the New York Times refers to as "one of the most controversial aspects of America's war in Vietnam."[333] As part of the program, the CIA used paramilitary units to get rid of hidden Communist spies throughout South

---

[331] "Interview with James Verlin Kimsey." Accessed May 26, 2022. https://memory.loc.gov/diglib/vhp-stories/loc.natlib.afc2001001.84178/mv0001001.stream?start=4.
[332] "Interview with James Verlin Kimsey." Accessed May 26, 2022. https://memory.loc.gov/diglib/vhp-stories/loc.natlib.afc2001001.84178/mv0001001.stream?start=4.
[333] Miller, Edward. "Opinion | Behind the Phoenix Program." *The New York Times*, December 30, 2017, sec. Opinion. https://www.nytimes.com/2017/12/29/opinion/behind-the-phoenix-program.html.

Vietnam. According to the Times, "Witnesses claimed that members of the program's teams and their American advisers routinely carried out torture, murders, and assassinations, accusations that American officials denied."[334] While most of the program's main operatives were Vietnamese, Americans in Vietnam created the program and made up much of the leadership. Kimsey joined the program in 1968, supervising operatives in the field all across Vietnam (he inspected Phoenix Program operations in 42 of the 44 Vietnamese provinces in just one year).[335]

Instead of commanding a small slice of land as he had in his first tour, Kimsey's new position gave him a better picture of the war as a whole: "The first tour was a worm's-eye view of the war," he remembers, "and the second was a bird's-eye view."[336] With his new role, Kimsey watched General Creighton Abrams and William Colby run the Vietnam War in person, getting a firsthand glimpse into the "frustrations and the disorganization" of America's position in Vietnam.[337] Despite this somewhat negative exposure and the questionable ethics of the Phoenix Program, Kimsey never became bitter with the war, and felt that he flourished in the environment. "I enjoyed the responsibility, I enjoyed the excitement," he recalls.[338] He thrived as a leader, reaching the rank of major as the war wound down, but refused

---

[334] Miller, Edward. "Opinion | Behind the Phoenix Program." *The New York Times*, December 30, 2017, sec. Opinion. https://www.nytimes.com/2017/12/29/opinion/behind-the-phoenix-program.html.
[335] "Interview with James Verlin Kimsey." Accessed May 26, 2022. https://memory.loc.gov/diglib/vhp-stories/loc.natlib.afc2001001.84178/mv0001001.stream?start=4.
[336] "Interview with James Verlin Kimsey." Accessed May 26, 2022. https://memory.loc.gov/diglib/vhp-stories/loc.natlib.afc2001001.84178/mv0001001.stream?start=4.
[337] "Interview with James Verlin Kimsey." Accessed May 26, 2022. https://memory.loc.gov/diglib/vhp-stories/loc.natlib.afc2001001.84178/mv0001001.stream?start=4.
[338] "Interview with James Verlin Kimsey." Accessed May 26, 2022. https://memory.loc.gov/diglib/vhp-stories/loc.natlib.afc2001001.84178/mv0001001.stream?start=4.

to become a "staff guy at the Pentagon" after the war ended.[339] "I could think of no worse thing to do with my life than that," he said of working a desk job at the Pentagon.[340] After serving for 8 years, Kimsey pulled strings with General Abrams to approve his resignation in order to avoid an assignment he might not like back home, ending his time with the military.[341]

Following his departure from the Army, Kimsey had $2,000 saved. With no idea what to do with his life post-military, he found himself walking around Washington, D.C. looking for real estate to buy. Eventually, he settled on building a bar in partnership with a real estate broker who would have his office above the bar. To make the business special, Kimsey came up with the idea of installing a New York Stock Exchange ticker tape machine in the bar so that people could watch the market over drinks. According to him, his "exchange bar" was the first of its kind in the world. He would go on to open up four more locations with the same gimmick, earning himself a pretty penny for a job he felt was easy compared to his time in the Army. Looking back, Kimsey notes how lucky he was that his venture into the risky bar business succeeded, calling himself "Mr. Magoo walking through the Valley of Death."[342]

After establishing his financial success with the exchange bars, Kimsey looked to establish himself in other areas. On the advice of a friend from West Point, Kimsey got involved with Bill von Meister, who he referred to at the time as "a guy

---

[339] "Interview with James Verlin Kimsey." Accessed May 26, 2022. https://memory.loc.gov/diglib/vhp-stories/loc.natlib.afc2001001.84178/mv0001001.stream?start=4.
[340] "Interview with James Verlin Kimsey." Accessed May 26, 2022. https://memory.loc.gov/diglib/vhp-stories/loc.natlib.afc2001001.84178/mv0001001.stream?start=4.
[341] "Interview with James Verlin Kimsey." Accessed May 26, 2022. https://memory.loc.gov/diglib/vhp-stories/loc.natlib.afc2001001.84178/mv0001001.stream?start=4.
[342] "Interview with James Verlin Kimsey." Accessed May 26, 2022. https://memory.loc.gov/diglib/vhp-stories/loc.natlib.afc2001001.84178/mv0001001.stream?start=4.

downloading video games over the telephone."[343] Together they ran Control Video, an early start-up online video game company which provided a predecessor to game-on-demand services for the Atari 2600 gaming console. Unfortunately for Kimsey, his partner was "a very smart, inventive kind of guy, and a good promoter, but he couldn't run anything. He sucked up a lot of money and venture capital."[344]

As Control Video floundered, Kimsey was also involved in starting a business bank, which he was trying to take public. As part of the process, the SEC asked if Kimsey had ever been the head of a company within two years of it going bankrupt. It was at this point that he knew that he had to turn Control Video around, or at least get it off his hands. First he tried to sell the farm to Apple: "I was trying to sell it to Apple," he remembers, "but Jobs and Scully were rolling around on the floor and I couldn't get their attention."[345] Instead, he ended up in a meeting with Commodore, one of the biggest early personal computer manufacturers. "I ended up talking to a guy at Commodore named Irving Gould who was the chairman at Commodore at the time, which was a billion-dollar company and the biggest presence in the home computer market. He had somebody in his outfit that had a scheme with a little company in Troy, New York called PlayNet, and we could mush this all together and start a new company," he recalls.[346] The two companies merged to form Quantum Computing Services in 1985, which would eventually become America Online – you likely know it as AOL – in 1990.

---

[343] "Interview with James Verlin Kimsey." Accessed May 26, 2022. https://memory.loc.gov/diglib/vhp-stories/loc.natlib.afc2001001.84178/mv0001001.stream?start=4.
[344] "Interview with James Verlin Kimsey." Accessed May 26, 2022. https://memory.loc.gov/diglib/vhp-stories/loc.natlib.afc2001001.84178/mv0001001.stream?start=4.
[345] "Interview with James Verlin Kimsey." Accessed May 26, 2022. https://memory.loc.gov/diglib/vhp-stories/loc.natlib.afc2001001.84178/mv0001001.stream?start=4.
[346] "Interview with James Verlin Kimsey." Accessed May 26, 2022. https://memory.loc.gov/diglib/vhp-stories/loc.natlib.afc2001001.84178/mv0001001.stream?start=4.

Kimsey headed Quantum Computing with Steve Case, with whom he had led Control Video. Because he was older and more credible, Kimsey focused on raising money. He helped build the board and build the investor group. "I focused on the marketing and strategic partners," he recalls of his time at Control Video.[347] At Quantum, the pair developed and sold user-friendly online programs for Commodore (Q-Link), Apple (AppleLink), and IBM (PCLink) computers before launching America Online, which provided users access to games, email, chat rooms, and some news articles.[348] Kimsey initially planned to get out of the business quickly, but things didn't exactly end up that way. "I told the people who put the money in, 'I'm gonna run this for a year, but we're going to have to find a real guy to do this, because I'm not a tech guy.' I ended up running it for 11 years," he remembers.[349]

In 1996, Kimsey finally made his departure from the company: "In '96 I decided it was time to back away (I get bored easily), so on a plane ride out to the West Coast I told Steve [Casey] I wanted to make him my successor because he lived and ate and breathed [AOL], I mean, he just loved it. And he was young enough. Of course my board was irate and wouldn't accept it but I knew him well enough and said, 'Well, that's what's going to happen one way or another.'"[350] He remembers the decision to

---

[347] Heath, Thomas. "James V. Kimsey, a Co-Founder of AOL, Dies at 76." *Washington Post*, March 4, 2016, sec. Capital Business. https://www.washingtonpost.com/business/capitalbusiness/james-v-kimsey-a-co-founder-of-aol-dies-at-76/2016/03/01/ed7e9eb6-dfcc-11e5-846c-10191d1fc4ec_story.html.
[348] Heath, Thomas. "James V. Kimsey, a Co-Founder of AOL, Dies at 76." *Washington Post*, March 4, 2016, sec. Capital Business. https://www.washingtonpost.com/business/capitalbusiness/james-v-kimsey-a-co-founder-of-aol-dies-at-76/2016/03/01/ed7e9eb6-dfcc-11e5-846c-10191d1fc4ec_story.html.
[349] "Interview with James Verlin Kimsey." Accessed May 26, 2022. https://memory.loc.gov/diglib/vhp-stories/loc.natlib.afc2001001.84178/mv0001001.stream?start=4.
[350] "Interview with James Verlin Kimsey." Accessed May 26, 2022. https://memory.loc.gov/diglib/vhp-stories/loc.natlib.afc2001001.84178/mv0001001.stream?start=4.

finally depart AOL as one of his most important acts: "I think one of the best things I ever did was let Steve run the company," he told The Washington Post in 1995. "Today that one decision to get out of the way makes me look like a genius."[351]

He left the company on course to reach its $224 billion-dollar peak in 2000.[352] His decision to leave also allowed him to avoid involvement in AOL's disastrous merger with Time-Warner. Providing perspective on the deal, Kimsey says, "Putting distribution, which was AOL, and content, which was Time-Warner, together, made sense on paper. But if I'd ever met Jerry Levin I would've never let that deal happen. I never fail to amuse myself by reminding Steve that it was the worst merger in American corporate history. Luckily I didn't get hurt by it too much."[353]

Post-AOL, Kimsey's largest mark on the world was his charity work. He funded new facilities at West Point and at both of his former high schools, and also created the Kimsey Foundation, focused on funding education and the arts. He was appointed chairman of the International Commission on Missing Persons in 2001 and became a board member at the Kennedy Center for the Performing Arts following a $10 million donation in 2006.[354] In his free time, he also performed in a band under

---

[351] Protess, Ben. "Jim Kimsey Dies at 76; AOL Co-Founder Influenced Generation of Net Providers." *The New York Times*, March 2, 2016, sec. Technology. https://www.nytimes.com/2016/03/03/technology/jim-kimsey-dies-at-76-aol-co-founder-influenced-generation-of-net-providers.html.
[352] Karaian, Jason. "By the Numbers: AOL Then and Now." Quartz. Accessed June 3, 2022. https://qz.com/403266/by-the-numbers-aol-then-and-now/.
[353] "Interview with James Verlin Kimsey." Accessed May 26, 2022. https://memory.loc.gov/diglib/vhp-stories/loc.natlib.afc2001001.84178/mv0001001.stream?start=4.
[354] Protess, Ben. "Jim Kimsey Dies at 76; AOL Co-Founder Influenced Generation of Net Providers." *The New York Times*, March 2, 2016, sec. Technology. https://www.nytimes.com/2016/03/03/technology/jim-kimsey-dies-at-76-aol-co-founder-influenced-generation-of-net-providers.html.

the name Verlin Jack. He passed away on March 1, 2016 of melanoma.[355]

---

[355] Heath, Thomas. "James V. Kimsey, a Co-Founder of AOL, Dies at 76." *Washington Post*, March 4, 2016, sec. Capital Business.
https://www.washingtonpost.com/business/capitalbusiness/james-v-kimsey-a-co-founder-of-aol-dies-at-76/2016/03/01/ed7e9eb6-dfcc-11e5-846c-10191d1fc4ec_story.html.

XI.

Richard Kinder

U.S. Army

Kinder Morgan

Richard Kinder was born on October 19, 1944. He was born in Cape Girardeau, Missouri to a middle class family. His father was an insurance salesman and his mother was a schoolteacher. "They believed in education and the American Dream," he remembers.[356] Growing up, Kinder was a go-getter: he was an Eagle Scout (the youngest in his region) and president of multiple clubs, participated in debate club, was sports editor for the school paper, and played tennis and baseball.

Following high school, Kinder attended the University of Missouri, receiving his bachelor's degree in American history in 1966 and JD in 1968. During high school, thanks to his time with the debate club, he knew that he wanted a law degree, as he enjoyed speaking and thinking on his feet. At college, he fancied himself a sort of politician. He was president of his fraternity, Sigma Nu, as well as the law school student body, and led other student activities. As for his political stance as a college student during the Vietnam War, Kinder quotes Churchill: "If you're not a liberal when you're 20, you have no heart. If you're not a conservative by the time you're 35, then you have no brain."[357] Despite this, he never participated in protests as a 20-something law student, having joined the military by 1968 – right when anti-Vietnam protests really began hitting their stride.

Kinder always wanted to serve in the military, viewing service as a part of citizenship. "I felt very strongly that ... it's difficult to have a meaningful role, particularly if you ever got into politics, and were arguing about whether to send somebody into harm's way, to not have served yourself. I'm a huge believer in the volunteer army, but one of its side effects is that, unlike 50 years ago, we no longer have the majority of Congressmen who have served themselves and know what war is all about and understand the military from the inside. We have a lot of people

---

[356] "OralHistory." Accessed September 9, 2022.
https://www.westpointcoh.org/interviews/service-as-a-component-of-citizenship-a-former-army-jag-on-business-and-philanthropy.
[357] "OralHistory." Accessed September 9, 2022.
https://www.westpointcoh.org/interviews/service-as-a-component-of-citizenship-a-former-army-jag-on-business-and-philanthropy.

who may pretend to understand it but I'm not sure that if you haven't served you really have as good an understanding," he said in an interview.[358] He originally wanted to serve as a "judge advocate" (essentially a military lawyer) after finishing his law degree, but got drafted during a break between his bachelor's and JD. To serve, he participated in JROTC during law school, earning his second lieutenant's commission by the time he graduated.

At the time, getting into the Judge Advocate General's (JAG) Corps was very competitive, but Kinder was lucky enough to receive a commission. He was faced with two options at this point: continue as a lieutenant with the military police for two years, or move on to the Army JAG Corps as a captain for four years. He chose to follow his aspirations and joined the JAG Corps. His service started in September of 1968, just after he graduated from law school in June. He headed to Fort Hamilton in New York after finishing a year of JAG school, helping notify the kin of soldiers lost in Vietnam as well as working as a survival assistance officer, reaching out to survivors of deceased veterans.

After almost a year of service in New York, Kinder headed to Vietnam on December 14, 1969 by way of a chartered plane out of San Francisco. He landed in the Vietnam city of Bien Hoa, where he was instructed to get off the plane quickly as the airstrip was often under mortar fire. He then headed to his assignment just outside of Saigon, where he worked with the U.S. Army Area Command, a collection of units that included a group that repaired all the U.S. helicopters in Vietnam. Kinder worked as part of a JAG group responsible for an area spanning from Da Nang to the Mekong Delta. He worked various court-martial cases, usually falling into one of three categories: drug offenses, incidents involving Vietnamese citizens, or violence within units against officers.

Kinder left Vietnam in 1970 by way of San Francisco, serving out the rest of his time with the JAG in Fort Leavenworth

---

[358] "OralHistory." Accessed September 9, 2022. https://www.westpointcoh.org/interviews/service-as-a-component-of-citizenship-a-former-army-jag-on-business-and-philanthropy.

in Kansas. Returning to the civilian world, his first job after the military was a position at a private practice. He worked there for a time before joining an energy company named Florida Gas Transmission, which owned a major natural gas pipeline stretching from Texas to Florida, as an attorney. The company was eventually bought by the Continental Group and went through a few transitions before being purchased by what would become controversial energy giant Enron. At Enron, Kinder served as general counsel beginning in 1980 before taking over pipeline operations, eventually rising through the ranks to become its president and COO by 1990. "I just got involved as a lawyer in making deals and helping out on business decisions, and I just decided I'd rather be in the chair making business decisions than just providing the legal drafting," he said of his transition from law to business.[359] He left the company in 1996 as his contract expired, looking to retire with the goal of skiing all the mountains in Colorado. His departure from the company was filled with corporate gossip – media reported that he'd stepped down after not receiving a promised promotion to the position of CEO, with CEO Kenneth Lay staying on as chairman.[360]

Soon after he left Enron, Kinder's old JAG officer friend William "Bill" Morgan approached him with a business opportunity. Together, they pooled resources in order to buy millions of dollars worth of older pipelines that Enron was selling, starting what would become energy infrastructure giant Kinder Morgan. With a base of infrastructure to profit off of, the company quickly grew from a small firm of 300 employees to an energy giant. Today, Kinder Morgan owns 83,000 miles of pipeline, bringing in revenues of $16.61 billion in 2021 as one of

---

[359] "OralHistory." Accessed September 9, 2022. https://www.westpointcoh.org/interviews/service-as-a-component-of-citizenship-a-former-army-jag-on-business-and-philanthropy.

[360] *The Anti-Enron In 1996, Rich Kinder lost out on the CEO job at Enron. So he left to start his own energy firm. Now he's a billionaire. Take that, Ken Lay! - November 24, 2003.* (n.d.). Retrieved September 23, 2022, from https://archive.fortune.com/magazines/fortune/fortune_archive/2003/11/24/353783/index.htm

North America's largest energy infrastructure companies.[361,362] The genius behind the company is that it's structured as a master limited partnership (MLP), distributing its cash flow to private investors, allowing it to pay back its backers while also dodge corporate tax rates.[363]

Today, Kinder remains the executive chairman of his company. He is one of America's richest individuals, with a net worth of roughly $6.9 billion.[364] His nonprofit, the Kinder Foundation, focuses on the Houston area, donating millions of dollars to local schools and funding local green development projects.[365]

---

[361] *Inline XBRL Viewer*. (n.d.). Retrieved September 23, 2022, from https://www.sec.gov/ix?doc=/Archives/edgar/data/1506307/000150630722000018/kmi-20211231.htm

[362] *Kinder Morgan's Biggest Win in 2016 So Far | The Motley Fool*. (n.d.). Retrieved September 23, 2022, from https://www.fool.com/investing/2016/09/13/kinder-morgans-biggest-win-in-2016-so-far.aspx

[363] *The Anti-Enron In 1996, Rich Kinder lost out on the CEO job at Enron. So he left to start his own energy firm. Now he's a billionaire. Take that, Ken Lay! - November 24, 2003*. (n.d.). Retrieved September 23, 2022, from https://archive.fortune.com/magazines/fortune/fortune_archive/2003/11/24/353783/index.htm

[364] *Richard Kinder*. (n.d.). Forbes. Retrieved September 23, 2022, from https://www.forbes.com/profile/richard-kinder/

[365] *Richard Kinder*. (n.d.). Forbes. Retrieved September 23, 2022, from https://www.forbes.com/profile/richard-kinder/

XII.

Gordon Logan

U.S. Air Force

Sport Clips

Gordon Logan was born in Sumter, South Carolina, in 1946. His father was a Scottish sawmill and furniture factory owner, and encouraged his son to pursue his own entrepreneurial journey, which Logan did with enthusiasm. At eight, he became a junk collector, selling old newspapers to moving companies (for packing material at a penny a pound) and discarded clothes hangers to dry cleaning operations. "I was one of the original recyclers," says Logan, who graduated to selling fire extinguishers and customized Christmas cards door-to-door. "It was about the money, but it was fun too."

Logan attended MIT from 1964 to 1968, earning himself a BS in Mechanical Engineering. Following graduation, Logan worked on a project by Dow Chemical and BASF developing carpet fibers before heading to Vietnam in 1969. His job had offered him an occupational deferment from the draft, but Logan chose to serve his country overseas instead, joining the Air Force for military pilot training. "A lot of my friends were getting drafted," he remembers. "I didn't feel right getting what I thought was a hokey deferment." He first went through officer training school at Lackland Air Force Base in San Antonio before heading to Georgia for pilot training at Moody Air Force Base. After earning his wings there, he traveled to Clark Air Force Base in the Philippines, the main Air Force base running C-130 transport aircraft into Southeast Asia. Pilots would fly from the Philippines to South Vietnam before serving a month in-country. Logan followed suit, getting refugees displaced by the conflict to safety. Instead of returning to his job quickly after serving in Vietnam, Logan stayed with the Air Force for five years after being drafted, flying C130 aircraft out of Texas as an Aircraft Commander. For several months a year, he flew on NATO support missions across Europe, the Middle East, and Southeast Asia. One mission involved flying supplies to Phnom Penh as the city was under siege by the Khmer Rouge in Cambodia, before the city fell in 1975.

Logan retired from the Air Force in 1974, but remained in the Air Force Reserves while attending classes at University of Pennsylvania's Wharton School, where he earned an MBA in

Accounting and Finance with the class of 1976. After graduating, he quickly moved to a consulting position with Pricewaterhouse in Houston, where he helped client companies manage their organizational structure, cost accounting systems, and payroll. Working with many other businesses, Logan began to want to run his own company, though he lacked experience. He wanted to join a franchise system in order to gain that experience: "In the consulting business you see a lot of businesses, but you don't really run a business," he recalls. "I thought it made sense to get into a franchise because you had an established business and marketing systems."

In 1978, Logan bought a franchise of Command Performance, a hair salon company. Unfortunately for him, he would not find the stability that he sought buying into the franchise. Command specialized in marketing, especially to a younger clientele, but it was a largely mismanaged venture. The company eventually went bankrupt in 1981, just three years after Logan bought in. Looking to retain his value after the bankruptcy, Logan joined a committee of franchise owners who negotiated with the company. They secured themselves a 40% share in the brand along with two seats on the board of directors and a reduction in royalty payments. The negotiations also made it harder for the company to terminate relationships with franchisees. This level of autonomy for franchise owners backfired, leading to inconsistent standards and pricing, with some locations charging $6 for haircuts while others charged $30. "I learned a lot about how not to run a franchise," Logan recalls of his time as a Command Performance franchisee. The brand changed hands multiple times after its bankruptcy, with Logan even becoming co-owner in 1991, but he also sold his control shortly after in order to start what would become Sport Clips.

During his time at Command Performance, Logan knew that his franchises had something that other hair salons didn't. "We had nice-looking up-to-date, hip salons. We're blasting rock 'n' roll and had a much younger look and feel than your typical salon. It was very successful at first" despite its flaws, he recalls.

While the business operation of Command Performance had deep issues, he felt he could take the idea of a hip, young salon and apply it to a market he'd had his eye on for a while: men. "Men reminisced about growing up, going to the barber shop with their dads, about the camaraderie and the banter, talking about sports and hunting and fishing," he says. He also had data supporting this, sourced from a market research firm he'd paid to survey men's thoughts on hair care. At this point, the neighborhood barbershops of generations past were fading out – "Men were being forced to go to salons, or to what were termed as family haircutters, like Fantastic Sam's or Great Clips or Supercuts," he recalls of the salon market at the time. The research firms also found that hair stylists were open to working on men's hair as the styles were simpler and easier to learn.

With a solid plan for his business as well as the support of his hair stylist wife, Logan opened the first Sport Clips in Austin, Texas in 1993. He planned for the business to grow into a franchise structure much like Command Performance, but this hope took time to come to fruition. The first franchisee was Ken Schiller, a former Nationwide Insurance franchise owner, bought into the business in 1995, two long years after Sport Clips' inception. "I believed in the concept," says Schiller, "I liked Gordon, his track record, his experience — I just believed that it was a good opportunity." His main two reasons for buying in were a strong business thesis – working in the underserved male hair care industry – as well as Sport Clips' offer to handle daily operations for franchisees (for a price), which allowed him to focus on other ventures. From there, Sport Clips continued to expand slowly. The company opened its fiftieth location after five years in 1998, and from there on its growth accelerated: by 2000, there were 100 locations open, and the company celebrated opening both its 400th and 500th locations in 2007. By 2012, the company expanded into Canada, and opened its 1,800th location in 2018.

Today, Sport Clips is one of the biggest brands in the salon industry, closing in on 1,900 franchises. To keep quality up and encourage sustainable growth, Logan has kept a rigid checklist of regulations for franchises since the business began. Prospective owners are interviewed and profiled to ensure that they will succeed as business owners within the Sport Clips ecosystem, and the company makes sure to treat its owners and employees correctly. The lack of inventory and training for individual franchises means there are fewer moving parts for franchisees to juggle, and the company even lets its managers slowly transition into full-time franchise ownership over time, meaning less opportunity for amateur mistakes.

In 2020, Logan stepped down as CEO of Sport Clips, naming his son Edward Logan as his successor. Today, the elder Logan serves as chairman of the board to Sport Clips and helps guide the business and its charitable works. In 2018, roughly 15% of the company's employees were veterans, and the company continues to donate millions of dollars to veterans' causes with a focus on education.

XIII.

Phyllis Newhouse

U.S. Army

Xtreme Solutions

This book has, so far, only featured male military veteran entrepreneurs. Why? Well, women have worked with the U.S. military in some capacity since the Revolutionary War, though mostly in very limited capacities – often unofficially serving as nurses or support staff. They were banned from many combat and officer roles until very recently, and still make up only a small portion of all service members in part due to the military's historical insistence on banning them from certain roles.

    Women were first allowed to serve openly in the military during World War I, though still in support roles. During World War II, even more women joined the military (still in clerical and nursing roles), making up just a fraction of all service members – roughly 350,000 women enlisted out of a total 16 million Americans who served. By 1948, just before the Korean War, President Harry S. Truman passed the Women's Armed Services Integration Act, allowing women to serve as full active duty service members in every branch of the military. Despite the progress, the bill still limited the number of women allowed to serve. Women were allowed to make up just 2% of each branch, with limits on how many women could become officers as well. They were also not allowed to serve in combat roles or command male service members. Roughly 120,000 women served in Korea, with many working as military police officers and engineers.

    During the Vietnam War, President Lyndon B. Johnson passed a bill allowing women to be promoted to general and flag ranks, and in 1972, women were finally allowed to command men. By the time of the Gulf War in 1990, 40,000 women were deployed in combat zones but still did not serve in direct combat roles. In 1994, President Bill Clinton rescinded a rule blocking women from serving in combat roles, allowing more women to serve as aviators and sailors (though a handful of women had served in those roles prior to the rule being lifted). Women were still banned from direct ground combat until 2013, when Defense Secretary Leon Panetta announced that all combat roles in the military would be available to women. In 2020, women made up around 16% of all military branches, with over 300,000 serving in Iraq and Afghanistan.[366]

With all of that information as background, Phyllis Newhouse's story is even more remarkable. An Army woman through and through, she served with the Army for 22 years. Her military resume includes reaching the rank of command sergeant major, specializing in national security, and even being chosen to establish the Cyber Espionage Task Force under Colin Powell.

Newhouse was born in Charlotte, North Carolina, in 1962 as the second-youngest in a family of 11 children.[367] Besides her 10 siblings, their packed household was also home to seven of her grandmother's children, who Phyllis' mother raised as her own children following the death of her mother – so Phyllis grew up not knowing that her "sisters" were, in fact, her aunts.[368] She describes her mother as "the first CEO I've ever met," and her father as a "disciplinarian" – qualities they needed to keep their big family in line.[369] Her father was also set on discovering his children's talents, and called Phyllis his "little soldier" and a "warrior" – shoes she sought to fill from a young age. She credits many of the lessons she learned as a kid for helping jump-start her career in the military.

She joined the military in 1978, inspired to enlist in part by a visit to see her sister who was stationed at Pope Air Force Base. At the base, she saw a group of female pilots getting out of their planes in their jumpsuits, and was taken in by how powerful they looked in their uniforms – as well as the fact that they were allowed to fly planes. "I had never seen women with

---

[366] Brookings. "Women Warriors: The Ongoing Story of Integrating and Diversifying the American Armed Forces," May 7, 2020. https://www.brookings.edu/essay/women-warriors-the-ongoing-story-of-integrating-and-diversifying-the-armed-forces/.

[367] *Exec. Profiles: Xtreme Solutions, Inc. CEO Phyllis Newhouse*, 2019. https://www.youtube.com/watch?v=PR0EyExp064.

[368] Magazine, ELYSIAN. "Phyllis Newhouse - Entrepreneur & Veteran." *ELYSIAN Magazine* (blog), December 12, 2017. https://readelysian.com/phyllis-newhouse-2/.

[369] *Phyllis Newhouse Is on a Mission to Empower Women Entrepreneurs*, 2021. https://www.youtube.com/watch?v=CTa917_Ft2M.

that level of command and authority and power and confidence. I was blown away," she recalls.[370] She left college early to join the Army, "intending to serve five years and see Europe" – though she ended up staying a bit longer than that.[371]

While stories about Newhouse's service are sparse due to the sensitive nature of much of her work in the military, she has given a few accounts of her time with the Army. Once she enlisted, she didn't find it hard to adapt to the military lifestyle. "Have you ever washed pots and dishes for 11 kids? It was a piece of cake compared with the military camp I was coming from," she said of the transition.[372] In her own words, Newhouse's first years in the military were spent proving her worth. She passed multiple data security aptitude tests soon after enlisting, setting herself up for her long military career in the national security lane. At her station in Fort Stewart, Georgia, she also heard that women rarely earned perfect scores on their physical aptitude tests – she then went on to earn a perfect 300 out of 300 on her physical tests every year.[373]

---

[370] Lagorio-Chafkin, Christine. "She's a Soldier and a Founder on a Singular Mission: Open as Many Doors as Possible for Women." Inc.com, September 28, 2021.
https://www.inc.com/magazine/202110/christine-lagorio-chafkin/phyllis-newhouse-xtreme-solutions-athena-leader-financial-empowerment-female-founders-2021.html.

[371] Newhouse, Phyllis. "She Was the Only Black Woman in the Room. So She Decided to Become the Best in the Business." Inc.com, September 3, 2021.
https://www.inc.com/magazine/202109/phyllis-newhouse/athena-technology-xtreme-solutions-only-black-woman-greatest.html.

[372] Lagorio-Chafkin, Christine. "She's a Soldier and a Founder on a Singular Mission: Open as Many Doors as Possible for Women." Inc.com, September 28, 2021.
https://www.inc.com/magazine/202110/christine-lagorio-chafkin/phyllis-newhouse-xtreme-solutions-athena-leader-financial-empowerment-female-founders-2021.html.

[373] Lagorio-Chafkin, Christine. "She's a Soldier and a Founder on a Singular Mission: Open as Many Doors as Possible for Women." Inc.com, September 28, 2021.
https://www.inc.com/magazine/202110/christine-lagorio-chafkin/phyllis-newhouse-xtreme-solutions-athena-leader-financial-empowerment-female-founders-2021.html.

The second period of her service saw Newhouse stationed abroad in Europe as she'd wanted. During this time, she began looking for more leadership roles. "I saw very few women in top ranks when I first went in," she remembers. "And so that gave me the desire to say, 'You know you can only make change when you're at the top.' So I strived to be a great leader because I knew that there were a lot of things in the military that needed to change, but you needed somebody who was willing to lead the military through change."[374] She worked out of Stuttgart, Germany, taking roles across Europe, including NATO command in Belgium. She grew her network of mentors and garnered more experience in preparation for her next period in the military.

The final leg in Newhouse's 22-year military journey began in 1996, when she was called back to the U.S. to be interviewed by Colin Powell for a new job opportunity. Though she wasn't the most qualified person for the job, Powell told her, "never look at the qualifications on a paper. Look at the greatest potential in a person and you will always get the best person."[375] He saw the potential in her and selected Newhouse to establish the Army's Cyber Espionage Task Force, a new apparatus linking the Army's cyber-defense efforts with those of other branches of the military. She successfully set up the task force, staffing and organizing the new group before leaving the military in 1999. She'd entered service as a private, and reached the rank of command sergeant major by the time she left, taking her from the bottom of the ladder all the way to the highest enlisted Army rank possible.

Back in the civilian world, Newhouse was already equipped with a plan. "The military is five years ahead of the

---

[374] *Phyllis Newhouse Is on a Mission to Empower Women Entrepreneurs*, 2021.
https://www.youtube.com/watch?v=CTa917_Ft2M.
[375] Lagorio-Chafkin, Christine. "She's a Soldier and a Founder on a Singular Mission: Open as Many Doors as Possible for Women." Inc.com, September 28, 2021.
https://www.inc.com/magazine/202110/christine-lagorio-chafkin/phyllis-newhouse-xtreme-solutions-athena-leader-financial-empowerment-female-founders-2021.html.

current trends in the market, so when I left the Pentagon I thought, 'I've already done this kind of work,'" she remembers. "Why not pursue a cybersecurity start-up?"[376] Even though the Pentagon had offered her a position as a senior-level advisor, she was dead set on starting her own business. "My reason for starting a business and becoming an entrepreneur was so compelling that failure was simply not an option," she said. "The idea that fueled me to start my business drives me to get up and go to work every day — that idea of continuing to serve. Our mission is to fight cybercrimes, attacks, and to protect our nation."[377]

Newhouse's cybersecurity and IT firm, Xtreme Solutions, began business soon after she left the Pentagon. Despite struggling due to her lack of commercial credit history or assets, as well as the stress of recently becoming a single parent for her infant son, Newhouse was able to secure enough cash to serve her first few clients using funding from a small credit facility, and the business eventually took off after a lot of elbow grease.[378] In April 2001, she visited AT&T's Atlanta headquarters, hoping to secure a contract to provide the funding she needed to hire her first employees. Without having any contacts at the company, she had the info of a cybersecurity and a research-and-development representative within 15 minutes of entering the lobby, and secured a contract (which required six

---

[376] "Phyllis W. Newhouse, XSI CEO, Named EY Entrepreneur of the Year- Technology Category Award Winner," April 3, 2018. https://www.xtremesolutions-inc.com/my-first-blog-post.
[377] "Phyllis W. Newhouse, XSI CEO, Named EY Entrepreneur of the Year- Technology Category Award Winner," April 3, 2018. https://www.xtremesolutions-inc.com/my-first-blog-post.
[378] "Phyllis W. Newhouse, XSI CEO, Named EY Entrepreneur of the Year- Technology Category Award Winner," April 3, 2018. https://www.xtremesolutions-inc.com/my-first-blog-post.

new hires) after just a few hours of negotiations.[379] Soon after, she signed a federal cybersecurity contract that would need a team of 24 people, and her business continued to grow from there. 18 months into the business, Xtreme Solutions was a 200-person company, and would continue to grow by at least 42% every year for the next eight years.[380] Currently, the company has employees in 46 states, over 30% of whom are veterans – though the rest of its information remains classified due to the nature of the cybersecurity sector.

While she had originally intended for Xtreme Solutions to serve mainly commercial clients, she soon realized that most of her business was coming from government contracts. Using this insight, she pivoted her company to focus on government deals, and Xtreme Solutions has become a nationwide industry leader. "I have learned to be incredibly flexible and trustworthy with my team, be accountable to make difficult decisions under pressure and exhibit strong organizational commitment always," she says. "As a leader, I think by taking on this leap of faith to start a business and scale, I have two of the most distinct qualities that entrepreneurs and service members share, and that's discipline and concentration. In scaling a business, I pride myself on the mindset of 'mission focus.'"[381]

Besides remaining flexible and faithful as a leader, Newhouse says she's learned some entrepreneurial lessons from

---

[379] Lagorio-Chafkin, Christine. "She's a Soldier and a Founder on a Singular Mission: Open as Many Doors as Possible for Women." Inc.com, September 28, 2021.
https://www.inc.com/magazine/202110/christine-lagorio-chafkin/phyllis-newhouse-xtreme-solutions-athena-leader-financial-empowerment-female-founders-2021.html.

[380] Lagorio-Chafkin, Christine. "She's a Soldier and a Founder on a Singular Mission: Open as Many Doors as Possible for Women." Inc.com, September 28, 2021.
https://www.inc.com/magazine/202110/christine-lagorio-chafkin/phyllis-newhouse-xtreme-solutions-athena-leader-financial-empowerment-female-founders-2021.html.

[381] "Phyllis W. Newhouse, XSI CEO, Named EY Entrepreneur of the Year- Technology Category Award Winner," April 3, 2018.
https://www.xtremesolutions-inc.com/my-first-blog-post.

her time in the military as well. "I think the U.S. military is often regarded as the 'greatest leadership institution in the world,'" she says. "This title is earned, in part, not for the structure of its teachings and practices, but rather for the mindset of those who lead and are led. I learned these lessons: To hold myself fully accountable for any and all actions of my team; to seek to motivate and uplift those around me, whether or not they are under my supervision; to outline our mission so it is clear to the team what our goal is and how we are going to get there; to surround myself with people who are better, smarter, faster or stronger in areas of business where I'm not as versed; and to delegate when a task doesn't fall under my core focus."

Newhouse has also found success outside of the cybersecurity industry. In 2020, she founded Athena Technology Acquisition Corp., a $250 million SPAC which IPO'd on the New York Stock Exchange.[382] When it IPO'd, Athena was the only Black woman-led SPAC out of 528 active SPACs – only 17 of those SPACs were led by women of any race. At the end of 2021, Athena merged with Heliogen, Inc., an AI-powered solar energy company.[383] She also founded another SPAC named ShoulderUp Technology Acquisition Corp. in 2021, which didn't end up merging with another company.

Newhouse has also founded a nonprofit organization named ShoulderUp alongside Hollywood star Viola Davis. The nonprofit offers mentorship and financial-literacy initiatives for young women in order to help them get a leg up in the world of business. ShoulderUp also encompasses ShoulderUp Ventures,

---

[382] McGrath, Maggie. "Exclusive: Phyllis Newhouse And Isabelle Freidheim Are Busting Up The SPAC Boys' Club By Bringing Athena To Market." Forbes. Accessed December 13, 2022.
https://www.forbes.com/sites/maggiemcgrath/2021/03/19/phyllis-newhouse-and-isabelle-freidheim-are-busting-up-the-spac-boys-club-by-bringing-athena-to-market/.

[383] Heliogen. "Heliogen, Inc. Announces Completion of Business Combination with Athena Technology Acquisition Corp." Heliogen, December 30, 2021.
https://heliogen.com/heliogen-inc-announces-completion-of-business-combination-with-athena-technology-acquisition-corporation/.

the first women-founded and women-led influencer fund that provides female investors financial opportunities and a wide portfolio of many different media, tech, and sports companies.

XIV.

Stephen Schwarzman

U.S. Army

Blackstone Group

Stephen Schwarzman was born on February 14, 1947 and grew up in Huntingdon Valley, Pennsylvania, as the oldest of three sons born to Arline and Joseph Schwarzman.[384] His father Joseph ran a dry goods store "that sort of looked like Bed, Bath and Beyond, but this was a long time ago and there was no Bed, Bath and Beyond," Schwarzman recalls.[385] He worked at this store starting at the age of 10, and within a few years realized just how successful his father's business could be. He pushed his father to expand the store into a national, or at least regional, chain, but he refused. "That's a bad idea," was his answer. "I'm very happy with my life as it is. I've got enough money to send you and your brothers to college. We've got a nice house and two cars. I don't want any more in life."[386] His father retired at the age of 70, selling the store to a buyer before it closed down 10 years later due to pressure from national chains like Bed, Bath and Beyond. "I admired him," Schwarzman recalls of his father. "He knew what he wanted and he achieved it. But that's not for me. I wanted a much bigger stage. I didn't know what it was, but I knew something had to be out there."[387]

He attended nearby Abington High School, where he ran track and played baseball. Despite his height (5'8"), Schwarzman found success in sports by practicing harder than everyone else, learning that by sheer effort, "you gain an advantage at the

---

[384] The New York Times. "WEDDINGS;Christine Hearst, S. A. Schwarzman," November 5, 1995, sec. Style. https://www.nytimes.com/1995/11/05/style/weddings-christine-hearst-s-a-schwarzman.html.
[385] Washington Post. "Transcript: The CEO Series: Steve Schwarzman," October 10, 2019. https://www.washingtonpost.com/washington-post-live/2019/10/10/transcript-ceo-series-steve-schwarzman/.
[386] "The Birthday Party | The New Yorker." Accessed March 17, 2023. https://web.archive.org/web/20200426055825/https://www.newyorker.com/magazine/2008/02/11/the-birthday-party-2.
[387] "The Birthday Party | The New Yorker." Accessed March 17, 2023. https://web.archive.org/web/20200426055825/https://www.newyorker.com/magazine/2008/02/11/the-birthday-party-2.

margin."[388] At one point, he broke his wrist during a fall at a cross-country race, but was so determined to set a record for the course that he just kept running with his wrist tucked by his side until he finished the race before promptly collapsing – he set the record, though. He graduated high school in 1965, and headed to Connecticut to continue his education at Yale.

At Yale, he made friends with students who matched his drive and ambition, as well as certain administrators and professors. "I've always been comfortable with people who run things, whether it was the principal of my high school or the president of the university," Schwarzman said of his relationships with school superiors. "I empathize with their problems, with their issues. I ask myself, How would I do that? It's very easy if you think about what they think. It comes naturally to me."[389] He joined the Skull and Bones secret society in his senior year, which allowed him to rub shoulders with many of the school's elite alumni, which eventually led him to pursue an MBA at Harvard Business School after he graduated from Yale in 1969 with a degree in Intensive Culture and Behavior, an interdisciplinary major.

Right out of school, Schwarzman joined Donaldson, Lufkin & Jenrette, a banking firm run by Yale alumni Bill Donaldson.[390] "It seemed fast-moving, intense," Schwarzman recalled. "Everyone seemed happy." When asked why he wanted to work at the firm, Schwarzman replied, "Mr. Donaldson, I don't even know what you do. But if you have such great-looking girls and intense guys then I want to do it."[391] His starting salary was

---

[388] "The Birthday Party | The New Yorker." Accessed March 17, 2023. https://web.archive.org/web/20200426055825/https://www.newyorker.com/magazine/2008/02/11/the-birthday-party-2.
[389] "The Birthday Party | The New Yorker." Accessed March 17, 2023. https://web.archive.org/web/20200426055825/https://www.newyorker.com/magazine/2008/02/11/the-birthday-party-2.
[390] "Stephen A. Schwarzman | Academy of Achievement." Accessed March 17, 2023. https://achievement.org/achiever/stephen-schwarzman/.
[391] "The Birthday Party | The New Yorker." Accessed March 17, 2023. https://web.archive.org/web/20200426055825/https://www.newyorker.com/magazine/2008/02/11/the-birthday-party-2.

$10,500 a year – "five hundred dollars more than anyone else in my class at Yale," he says. Despite enjoying his work and wanting to go into finance later in life, he felt out of his depth at the firm, leaving after six months. When he asked Donaldson why he'd bet on hiring him straight out of college, Donaldson replied, "One day you'll be the head of this firm. It's my instinct. You have something special and I want to bet on it."[392]

Taking a break from working, Schwarzman applied to and was accepted at Harvard Business School. He deferred his admission for a year and joined the Army Reserves to fulfill his service requirement. With the Army, he trained at Fort Polk, Louisiana, where his unit was consistently underfed. When he brought up the issue with a colonel, he got shot down. Instead of giving up, he continued pushing the issue with his superiors, eventually leading to the discovery of a ring of officers that were stealing food to sell off base. After saving his unit's food supply, he wrapped up his training requirement and returned to civilian life. He attended Harvard Business School – which he found boring, though he did meet his wife there – and graduated with an MBA in 1972.[393]

He returned to the world of finance after graduation, earning himself a position at Lehman Brothers. He felt an affinity for the financial giant, which he described as "full of interesting characters, ex-CIA agents, ex-military, strays from the oil industry, family friends and randoms."[394] He quickly shot up the ranks at Lehman's mergers and acquisitions division, eventually becoming a partner after just six years and a managing director

---

[392] "The Birthday Party | The New Yorker." Accessed March 17, 2023. https://web.archive.org/web/20200426055825/https://www.newyorker.com/magazine/2008/02/11/the-birthday-party-2.
[393] "YAHOO FINANCE PRESENTS: How Stephen Schwarzman Built a Private Equity Empire," September 17, 2019. https://finance.yahoo.com/news/blackstone-ceo-steve-schwarzman-on-what-it-takes-100536957.html.
[394] "Stephen A. Schwarzman, the Billionaire Who Built Blackstone," March 13, 2022. https://fintechmagazine.com/venture-capital/stephen-a-schwarzman-the-billionare-who-built-blackstone.

by 31.[395,396] CEO Peter Peterson, who would go on to found The Blackstone Group with Schwarzman, described Scharzman as "extremely gifted, probably one of the two or three most gifted people I've met in the M. & A. world. More important, he had balance. He could make the major judgment calls. He knew when a C.E.O. needed to be called. He could gain their confidence better than anyone. I could bring in the business, but I couldn't implement it. He was great at this, great to work with. He'd carry out the deal, and keep me informed."[397]

In 1985, Schwarzman and Peterson left Lehman following a leadership schism. They pooled their wealth and finance savvy to form The Blackstone Group, their mergers & acquisitions venture, with seed capital of $400,000.[398] The name Blackstone came from a multilingual combination of their names: Black, (schwarz in German) and stone (petros in Greek).[399] The pair quickly realized that the uncertain world of M&A wasn't for them, and decided to pivot the firm towards private equity. They weathered the collapse of the junk-bond market, the savings-and-loan crisis, and the 1990-91 recession all in quick succession, building out their business' reputation by investing in real estate and providing strictly advisory services.

In just a few years, the firm gained investor confidence, carving out a reputation in the private equity world as a company

---

[395] "Stephen A. Schwarzman, the Billionaire Who Built Blackstone," March 13, 2022. https://fintechmagazine.com/venture-capital/stephen-a-schwarzman-the-billionare-who-built-blackstone.

[396] "The Birthday Party | The New Yorker." Accessed March 17, 2023. https://web.archive.org/web/20200426055825/https://www.newyorker.com/magazine/2008/02/11/the-birthday-party-2.

[397] "The Birthday Party | The New Yorker." Accessed March 17, 2023. https://web.archive.org/web/20200426055825/https://www.newyorker.com/magazine/2008/02/11/the-birthday-party-2.

[398] "Private Equity Power List | 1 | FORTUNE." Accessed March 25, 2023. https://money.cnn.com/galleries/2007/fortune/0702/gallery.powerlist.fortune/index.html.

[399] "The Birthday Party | The New Yorker." Accessed March 17, 2023. https://web.archive.org/web/20200426055825/https://www.newyorker.com/magazine/2008/02/11/the-birthday-party-2.

that specialized in non-hostile takeovers. Blackstone eventually secured a $850 million round of private funding from multiple investors, including the Prudential Insurance Company, Nikko Securities, and the General Motors pension fund.[400] This allowed the company a seat at the big boys' table, and it soon brokered Sony's purchase of CBS Corporation in 1988.[401] Blackstone had quickly become a force to be reckoned with in the world of private equity.

However, things aren't always that easy in the world of finance, especially if you grow a big head from years of sustained success. For Blackstone's third major investment, the firm had its sights set on Edgcomb Steel, a steel distribution company. While Schwarzman supported the investment, one of Blackstone's partners was not so keen, warning him that the steel company "was going to go bankrupt."[402] Schwarzman wasn't buying it. "I said 'Why is that?' He said they look like they're making money, 'but it's just inventory profits," he recalls. "Steel goes up; steel goes down. When it's going up ... they'll do really well. That's where we are now. When it goes down, it will all reverse and you won't be able to pay your principal in interest and it will go broke.'"[403] Shortly after he unilaterally signed off on the investment, the firm lost all of its investments in the

---

[400] Wayne, Leslie. "A Big Fund Ready to Capitalize on Hard Times." *The New York Times*, November 13, 1987, sec. Business.
https://www.nytimes.com/1987/11/13/business/a-big-fund-ready-to-capitalize-on-hard-times.html.

[401] Boyer, Peter J. "Sony and CBS Records: What a Romance!" *The New York Times*, September 18, 1988, sec. Magazine.
https://www.nytimes.com/1988/09/18/magazine/sony-and-cbs-records-what-a-romance.html.

[402] Imbert, Fred. "Blackstone CEO Steve Schwarzman Recounts the Most 'disastrous' Investment He Ever Made." CNBC, September 19, 2019.
https://www.cnbc.com/2019/09/19/blackstone-ceo-recounts-the-most-disastrous-investment-he-ever-made.html.

[403] Imbert, Fred. "Blackstone CEO Steve Schwarzman Recounts the Most 'disastrous' Investment He Ever Made." CNBC, September 19, 2019.
https://www.cnbc.com/2019/09/19/blackstone-ceo-recounts-the-most-disastrous-investment-he-ever-made.html.

company, and Schwarzman had to tell his clients what he'd done with their money.

Besides this bump, the company slowly but surely grew. The firm began investing in hedge funds, focusing more on real estate, and continuing its private equity ventures. By 2007, Blackstone introduced its IPO at $31 a share, valuing the company at $33.48 billion. Schwarzman and Peterson racked up $2.4 billion between them in the offering, with Schwarzman retaining a 23% stake in the company, valued at $7.74 billion.[404] Today, Blackstone is the largest alternative investment company in the world, with assets under management coming in at $951 billion.[405]

In 2020, Schwarzman revealed that he'd signed the giving pledge, promising to donate the majority of his wealth to philanthropic causes.[406] He's donated hundreds of millions of dollars to hospitals, schools, and even the New York Public Library. He's also created the Schwarzman Scholars, a scholarship program that provides students with the opportunity to attend a one-year fully-funded master's degree leadership program at Tsinghua University, China's top university.[407] He continues to run Blackstone to this day, signing off on all checks over $250,000, and retains a net worth of roughly $27.6 billion.

---

[404] Reuters. "Blackstone Raises $4.1 Billion," June 22, 2007, sec. Global Markets.
https://www.reuters.com/article/us-blackstone-ipo-idUSN2136246820070622.
[405] Blackstone. "Blackstone's Third Quarter 2022 Supplemental Financial Data," October 20, 2022.
https://www.blackstone.com/wp-content/uploads/sites/2/2022/10/Blackstone3Q22SupplementalFinancialData.pdf.
[406] "Blackstone CEO Stephen Schwarzman Commits to Donating the Majority of His Wealth to Charity | CNN Business." Accessed March 25, 2023.
https://www.cnn.com/2020/02/05/business/blackstone-ceo-giving-pledge/index.html.
[407] Giving Pledge. "Stephen A. Schwarzman - The Giving Pledge." Accessed March 25, 2023.
https://givingpledge.org/pledger?pledgerId=398.

XV.
Charlie Munger
U.S. Army
Berkshire Hathaway

The history of the Munger family stretches back all the way back to a group of early British settlers who helped set up the colonies in New England. They made their way to England from Germany, where the name Munger originated from monger – a person who sells commodities.[408] The first American Munger – Nicholas Munger – reached the shores of the New World in 1637. Nicholas attempted to begin a new life in Guilford, Connecticut, but the ground there proved inhospitable to crops, and subsequent generations of the Munger clan moved further west until one generation ended up in Nebraska.

Charlie Munger was the son of Alfred C. Munger, an attorney, and Florence "Toody" Russell Munger, the well-educated daughter of the wealthy and politically connected Russell family, in Omaha, Nebraska. He and his two sisters, Mary and Carol, all attended nearby Dundee Elementary School before graduating to Central High School, which at the time was a nationally ranked top-25 college preparatory school. Interestingly, Warren Buffett's siblings all went to the same schools as the Mungers, though Warren himself attended schools in Washington, D.C. in order to stay near his father, a congressman.

Throughout his student years, Munger wasn't much of an athlete, but did gain popularity thanks to his passion for books, his hobbies, and his friends. "He was always gregarious, friendly, social," remembers his sister Carol. "He was interested in science, almost anything – he had a curious mind."[409] Charlie grew into a star student thanks to his family's obsession with reading. "Charlie was so lively that you could hardly miss him," remembers his sister. "He was up to something all the time. Occasionally he got into a scrape with his teachers, as he was too

---

[408] Lowe, Janet. *Damn Right!: Behind the Scenes with Berkshire Hathaway Billionaire Charlie Munger.* 1st edition. Wiley, 2007.
[409] Lowe, Janet. *Damn Right!: Behind the Scenes with Berkshire Hathaway Billionaire Charlie Munger.* 1st edition. Wiley, 2007.

independent minded to bow down to meet certain teachers' expectations."[410]

While his younger years were filled with hobbies, learning, and friends, Charlie also learned a few life lessons early on. He grew up during the Great Depression, and though his family was relatively well off, he chose to work to help out however he could. One of his first jobs was at Buffett & Son, a grocery store owned by the family of Charlie's future business partner and business mogul Warren Buffett. Charlie recalled his time at the store, remembering that he "slaved" at the store every Saturday. "You were just goddamn busy from the first hour of morning until night," he said.[411] For his labor, Warren Buffett's Grampa Ernest paid Charlie two dollars for every twelve hours of labor, and also made his employees bring in two pennies to cover their Social Security contributions. He also gave out lectures on the evils of socialism, though those were free.

Following the Great Depression, or perhaps curing it, World War II reared its ugly head. Right as the Munger children were heading off to college, conflict in Europe began, eventually leading to the U.S. being dragged into the war. Charlie headed to the University of Michigan as a 17-year old in 1941 for his degree in mathematics, but his first year of college was interrupted by the attack on Pearl Harbor in December of his first semester. While he stayed at school for a while after, he eventually joined the Armed Forces in 1943, just a few days before his 19th birthday. Throughout his schooling, Charlie was a member of the ROTC, so he was already bored of marching and the like. Instead of joining the infantry, the young man joined the Army Air Corps.

He went through Army basic training in Utah as an ordinary soldier before taking the Army General Classification test. Charlie scored 149 on the assessment, well above the 120 points necessary to become an officer. After being promoted to

---

[410] Lowe, Janet. *Damn Right!: Behind the Scenes with Berkshire Hathaway Billionaire Charlie Munger*. 1st edition. Wiley, 2007.
[411] Lowenstein, Roger. *Buffett: The Making of an American Capitalist*. Reprint edition. Random House, 2013.

Second Lieutenant, Charlie was soon sent to the University of New Mexico in Albuquerque before making his way to the California Institute of Technology in Pasadena, one of the nation's top science universities, to train as a meteorologist. It was there that he met a girl named Nancy, whom he quickly married and began a family with. After completing his training at CalTech, Munger headed off to Pasadena's polar opposite in terms of weather – Alaska. There, he watched as World War II's casualties piled up and thanked his lucky stars. "I don't think I knew well 15 people who died in World War II," he remembers. "It wasn't like a whole generation of young men died, as the Europeans did in World War I or the Americans in the Civil War. I never got near military action. I was stationed in Nome. I couldn't have gotten further from the action."[412]

22-year-old Munger left the military in 1946 with an education under his belt and his application to Harvard Law school already submitted. He was almost rejected from the school despite his father's alumni status, only barely making it in with the help of a family friend named Roscoe Pound. During his first year, Charlie placed second in his class, but he felt out of place academically. "I came to Harvard Law School very poorly educated, with desultory work habits and no college degree," he remembers.[413] Nonetheless, he graduated magna cum laude with a Juris Doctor in 1948.

After graduating, Munger moved with his family to Los Angeles despite his family's doubts. His father had considered a move to L.A. following World War I, but decided against it, declaring, "There's no future in this town," before landing in the Midwest. However, the younger Munger saw opportunity in the growing city, especially with his young wife's entrepreneurial family, and his father eventually approved of his move. Munger passed the California Bar in 1949, joining the law firm of Wright & Garrett that same year. He began saving up his salary of $275 a

---

[412] Lowe, Janet. *Damn Right!: Behind the Scenes with Berkshire Hathaway Billionaire Charlie Munger*. 1st edition. Wiley, 2007.
[413] Lowe, Janet. *Damn Right!: Behind the Scenes with Berkshire Hathaway Billionaire Charlie Munger*. 1st edition. Wiley, 2007.

month, providing for his family and expanding his network of business contacts in Southern California.

While things in L.A. started out sunny for the Mungers, their family situation took a turn for the worse, even as the U.S. experienced its post-World War II boom. Charlie and Nancy divorced in 1953, a time where divorce was extremely uncommon. As their daughter Molly recalls, "They fought, yelled at each other. It was abundantly clear they weren't happy," but when it became fully clear to the young couple that things just weren't going to work out, they reassured each other and their children that everything would be alright. "They handled themselves in a way that was exemplary," she recalls. "They said all the right things. We're not happy with each other. We need to be apart. We love you guys. It won't affect our relationship with you."[414] Despite those sentiments, Charlie was cleaned out in the split. Nancy kept the kids and their South Pasadena house, relegating her husband to visits on the weekends and a "dreadful" bachelor pad at the local University Club.[415]

Over the next few years, Munger collected his paychecks from his day job at the law firm, and began investing in various ventures around L.A. In one instance, he invested in a cathode ray recording oscillograph business with a friend, only to have the technology made quickly obsolete by magnetic tape recording technology. After that, he remembers, "I never went back to the high-tech mode. I tried it once and found it to have many problems. I was like Mark Twain's cat that, after a bad experience, never again sat on a hot stove or on a cold stove, either."[416]

In 1959, his father died. Munger headed back to Omaha to attend his funeral and spend time with his family, and it was

---

[414] Lowe, Janet. *Damn Right!: Behind the Scenes with Berkshire Hathaway Billionaire Charlie Munger.* 1st edition. Wiley, 2007.
[415] For?, But What. "Takeaway Tuesday - Facing Adversity with Charlie Munger." Accessed December 2, 2022. https://newsletter.butwhatfor.com/p/takeaway-tuesday-facing-adversity.
[416] Lowe, Janet. *Damn Right!: Behind the Scenes with Berkshire Hathaway Billionaire Charlie Munger.* 1st edition. Wiley, 2007.

then when he crossed paths with Warren Buffett, the grandson of the grocery store owner he'd worked for as a kid. The two instantly hit it off. "About five minutes into it, Charlie was sort of rolling on the floor laughing at his own jokes, which is exactly the same thing I did," recalls Buffett. "I thought, 'I'm not going to find another guy like this.' And we just hit it off."[417] From there, the pair stayed in touch but headed their separate ways, Munger continuing his law career and Buffett building his investment firm.

By 1961, Munger began investing in real estate as L.A. continued to grow. In 1962, he founded and worked as a real estate attorney at Munger, Tolles & Olson, which remains one of the nation's top law firms today. He also founded Wheeler, Munger, and Company, a securities firm, that same year with a poker buddy, and began trying his hand at the Pacific Coast Stock Exchange. By 1965, Munger was so invested in investing that he stopped practicing law, though he still retained an office and consulting position at his law firm.[418] The law firm had granted him many key connections: Rod Hills, a founding partner, would later become SEC chairman, and Warren Buffett and the collection of companies that would become Berkshire Hathaway were also clients of Munger, Tolles & Olson.[419] Munger stayed with Wheeler, Munger, and Co. until the 1973-1974 stock market downturn, when the firm took big hits in consecutive years, losing 32% in 1973 and 31% in 1974.[420]

---

[417] Stankiewicz, Kevin. "Buffett Reflects on His First Meeting with Munger: 'I'm Not Going to Find Another Guy like This.'" CNBC, June 30, 2021.
https://www.cnbc.com/2021/06/29/buffett-reflects-on-his-first-meeting-with-munger-im-not-going-to-find-another-guy-like-this.html.
[418] "Seeking Wisdom from the Early - GuruFocus.Com." Accessed March 17, 2023.
https://www.gurufocus.com/news/249886/seeking-wisdom-from-the-early-charlie-munger-.
[419] Lowe, Janet. *Damn Right!: Behind the Scenes with Berkshire Hathaway Billionaire Charlie Munger*. 1st edition. Wiley, 2007.
[420] Lowe, Janet. *Damn Right!: Behind the Scenes with Berkshire Hathaway Billionaire Charlie Munger*. 1st edition. Wiley, 2007.

During his time at the Pacific Coast Stock Exchange, Munger of course continued husting on the side. By this time, Buffett had long since become the chairman of Berkshire Hathaway, a textile company that would eventually become one of the most famous investing firms in the world. Munger and Buffett slowly bought up portions of Blue Chip Stamps, a company which issued trading stamps to merchants. The pair eventually gained a controlling interest in the company by the early 70s, with their eyes on the large pool of cash in its float account due to a difference in the amount of stamps issued and the amount of stamps redeemed. They then set about using this capital by snapping up various companies they saw as good investments. Operating as the majority owners of Blue Chip, they bought up multiple companies including See's Candy, The Buffalo Evening News, and Wesco Financial.[421] Through some legally-necessary reorganization, Berkshire Hathaway became the owner of Blue Chip and all the companies it had gobbled up, with Munger gaining a position as the vice chairman of it all in 1978.

From there, Berkshire grew quickly. Though the company's main capital comes from its control of various insurance firms including GEICO, it also gained positions in a wide range of companies including Nebraska Furniture Mart, ABC, Gillette, USAir, SAFECO Corporation, Champion International, and Coca-Cola. Through the 90s, Berkshire further expanded its reputation and holdings, becoming one of the biggest and most respected companies in the world by 2007.[422] At the end of 2022, Berkshire held almost $1 trillion in total assets; was the largest shareholder in American Express, Bank of America, Chevron, Coca-Cola, HP, Moody's, Occidental, and

---

[421] Lowe, Janet. *Damn Right!: Behind the Scenes with Berkshire Hathaway Billionaire Charlie Munger*. 1st edition. Wiley, 2007.
[422] "Action 3 News - Omaha, Nebraska News, Weather, and Sports | Warren Buffett's Berkshire Hathaway Named Most Respected Company," December 12, 2007.
https://web.archive.org/web/20071212120003/http://www.action3news.com/Global/story.asp?S=7081357&nav=menu550_2.

Paramount Global; and held cash and cash equivalents of $128.6 billion.

In 2023, Munger reportedly had a net worth of $2.2 billion.[423] Outside of business, the now-99-year-old has been a champion of various social causes, including abortion rights and healthcare access. He's donated hundreds of millions of dollars to different universities, sometimes leveraging his gifts to pursue his interest in architecture, and has given even more to various organizations he's interacted with over the years.

Munger and his investing partner remain friends to this day. "Charlie's never shaded anything he's told me in terms of presenting it to me in a different way than reality, or he's never done anything I've seen that's self-serving in terms of being a partner in any kind of way," Buffett said in an interview with CNBC.[424] "He makes me better than I would otherwise be and I don't want to disappoint him."

"You had the same thing, in reverse," Munger replied.

---

[423] Forbes. "Charles Munger." Accessed November 4, 2022. https://www.forbes.com/profile/charles-munger/.

[424] Jr, Tom Huddleston. "Warren Buffett and Charlie Munger: 'We Made a Lot of Money' but Here's 'What We Really Wanted.'" CNBC, June 30, 2021. https://www.cnbc.com/2021/06/30/buffett-and-munger-this-is-what-we-really-wanted-more-than-money.html.

XVI.

Jack Taylor

U.S. Navy

Enterprise Rent-A-Car

Jack Taylor, founder of Enterprise Rent-A-Car, was born on April 14, 1922 in St. Louis, Missouri, the first son of Melbourne Martling Taylor and Dorothy Crawford Taylor.[425] His brother Paul, who would help him expand Enterprise in the 1980s, was born a year later on November 19, 1923.[426] Early on, Jack attended Clayton High in St. Louis, where he recalls he was "a very callow youth" with "no direction," though he was passable at sports, running the 100-meter dash and playing basketball.[427,428] His status as a poor student continued into college: Taylor first attended Westminster College in Fulton, Missouri, for a brief stint before moving back home to attend Washington University in St. Louis.[429] "[I] did not do well, was not a good student," he remembers of his two semesters as a college student.[430] Luckily for his GPA, he remembers, the Japanese bombing of Pearl Harbor "saved me from any further

---

[425] Holdings, Enterprise. "Jack Crawford Taylor: War Hero, Business Leader, Philanthropist." Accessed June 17, 2022.
https://www.prnewswire.com/news-releases/jack-crawford-taylor-war-hero-business-leader-philanthropist-300293567.html.
[426] archive.ph. "Paul Taylor: Helped Brother Build Enterprise Leasing, the Nation's La...," April 15, 2013. https://archive.ph/iGybF.
[427] Jr, Robert D. Hershey. "Jack Taylor, Founder of Enterprise Rent-A-Car, Dies at 94." *The New York Times*, July 3, 2016, sec. Business.
https://www.nytimes.com/2016/07/03/business/jack-taylor-founder-of-enterprise-rent-a-car-dies-at-94.html
[428] Winkler, David F. "NHF Oral History Program | LT Jack C. Taylor," September 2001.
https://www.navyhistory.org/wp-content/uploads/2011/04/Jack-Taylor-Oral-History.pdf.
[429] Holdings, Enterprise. "Jack Crawford Taylor: War Hero, Business Leader, Philanthropist." Accessed June 17, 2022.
https://www.prnewswire.com/news-releases/jack-crawford-taylor-war-hero-business-leader-philanthropist-300293567.html.
[430] Winkler, David F. "NHF Oral History Program | LT Jack C. Taylor," September 2001.
https://www.navyhistory.org/wp-content/uploads/2011/04/Jack-Taylor-Oral-History.pdf.

educational opportunities," and he enlisted in the Army soon after the attack.[431]

At first, Taylor wanted to join the Army Air Corps. "I knew I wanted to fly. Don't ask me why. I'd never been up in an airplane at this point," he remembers.[432] His application process went well until his physical, when he told the doctor that he had hay fever. Unfortunately for him, Army pilots aren't allowed to fly with hay fever, and his application to the program was rejected. He headed back home, depressed, until a friend recommended he apply to fly for the Navy instead. Luckily, the Navy doctors never asked about hay fever as part of their process, and Taylor was accepted as a volunteer cadet through the Navy's V-5 pilot program.[433]

Though he was accepted as a pilot in March of 1942, Taylor's active duty started in December. That month, he was brought out to Kratz Field near St. Louis, where he learned to fly on Piper J-3 Cubs, general-use aircraft deployed by the military for reconnaissance and training.[434] After learning the basics of piloting at Kratz, he headed to Iowa Pre-Flight, a cadet school commissioned at the University of Iowa during World War 2.[435]

---

[431] Jr, Robert D. Hershey. "Jack Taylor, Founder of Enterprise Rent-A-Car, Dies at 94." *The New York Times*, July 3, 2016, sec. Business.
https://www.nytimes.com/2016/07/03/business/jack-taylor-founder-of-enterprise-rent-a-car-dies-at-94.html

[432] Winkler, David F. "NHF Oral History Program | LT Jack C. Taylor," September 2001.
https://www.navyhistory.org/wp-content/uploads/2011/04/Jack-Taylor-Oral-History.pdf.

[433] Winkler, David F. "NHF Oral History Program | LT Jack C. Taylor," September 2001.
https://www.navyhistory.org/wp-content/uploads/2011/04/Jack-Taylor-Oral-History.pdf.

[434] "Piper J-3," March 3, 2006.
https://web.archive.org/web/20060303180134/http://www.nasm.si.edu/research/aero/aircraft/piperj3.htm.

[435] Mather, Victor. "The Best College Football Team You've Probably Never Heard Of." *The New York Times*, August 21, 2017, sec. Sports.
https://www.nytimes.com/2017/08/21/sports/ncaafootball/the-best-college-football-team-youve-probably-never-heard-of.html.

There, he went through basic training. "A third of the day was military training, a third of the day was class training, and a third of the day was athletics," Taylor reminisces.[436] "Every Saturday you had to run an obstacle course, and if you didn't do it in a certain amount of time you had to come back and run it Sunday. I remember guys running that obstacle course and ending up throwing up, they tried so hard. It was tough training. Iowa Pre-Flight was tough."

From Iowa Pre-Flight, Taylor's training took him to Glenview Naval Air Station near Chicago. He trained on Naval Aircraft Factory N3N planes for 50 hours there, becoming accustomed to planes larger than the Piper J-3 Cubs he'd first learned to fly on, before moving on to train at Naval Air Station Corpus Christi in Texas, where he continued his long pilot training. This time he trained to fly Vultee Vindicators and SNJ-4s, which were closer tom combat aircraft than the light planes he had trained on previously.[437] He passed all his tests at Corpus Christi, receiving his wings in December of 1943. " I was a good pilot," he recalls. "I had quick reflexes and good depth perception, and I think that my instructors said: 'He's a pretty good pilot.'"[438] Because of his skill, he was assigned to become a fighter pilot, which meant another round of training at Vero Beach Naval Air Station in Florida.[439] At Vero Beach, he finally

---

[436] Winkler, David F. "NHF Oral History Program | LT Jack C. Taylor," September 2001.
https://www.navyhistory.org/wp-content/uploads/2011/04/Jack-Taylor-Oral-History.pdf.
[437] Winkler, David F. "NHF Oral History Program | LT Jack C. Taylor," September 2001.
https://www.navyhistory.org/wp-content/uploads/2011/04/Jack-Taylor-Oral-History.pdf.
[438] Winkler, David F. "NHF Oral History Program | LT Jack C. Taylor," September 2001.
https://www.navyhistory.org/wp-content/uploads/2011/04/Jack-Taylor-Oral-History.pdf.
[439] Winkler, David F. "NHF Oral History Program | LT Jack C. Taylor," September 2001.
https://www.navyhistory.org/wp-content/uploads/2011/04/Jack-Taylor-Oral-History.pdf.

got to fly a real fighter plane, the Grumman F6F Hellcat. Now learning to fly the plane he'd use on the battlefield, Taylor went through a three-month operational training in Florida before heading to the Great Lakes for his carrier qualifications. On Lake Michigan, he learned how to launch from and land on carriers, earning his qualifications after three launches.

Finally, Taylor was ready to be deployed. He headed to Hawaii by way of Southern California, joining the U.S.S. Essex as part of the fighter squadron, replacing pilots lost just days before during the Great Marianas Turkey Shoot in June of 1944.[440] On the Essex, Taylor was a member of Carrier Air Group 15, led by Commander David McCampbell, the Navy's all-time leading flying ace with 34 aerial victories.[441] During his time with the Essex, Taylor downed two Japanese planes and ran multiple missions, participating in Battle of the Philippine Sea and the invasion of Guam before the ship was sent back to port to resupply in October.[442] Taylor then joined the U.S.S. Enterprise, participating in the Formosa Air Battle, where he downed two more Japanese planes, and the Battle of Leyte Gulf, where he participated in the sinking of the Japanese superbattleship Musashi.[443] Eventually he rejoined the reprovisioned U.S.S. Essex, flying a few more missions with the carrier before his squadron was relieved of duty on November 10, 1944 after

---

[440] Winkler, David F. "NHF Oral History Program | LT Jack C. Taylor," September 2001.
https://www.navyhistory.org/wp-content/uploads/2011/04/Jack-Taylor-Oral-History.pdf.
[441] "McCampbell, David." Accessed July 1, 2022.
http://public1.nhhcaws.local/our-collections/photography/us-people/m/mccampbell-david.html.
[442] Winkler, David F. "NHF Oral History Program | LT Jack C. Taylor," September 2001.
https://www.navyhistory.org/wp-content/uploads/2011/04/Jack-Taylor-Oral-History.pdf.
[443] Winkler, David F. "NHF Oral History Program | LT Jack C. Taylor," September 2001.
https://www.navyhistory.org/wp-content/uploads/2011/04/Jack-Taylor-Oral-History.pdf.

serving for four and a half months.[444] Roughly two weeks after he left the carrier, the Essex's fighter ready room was destroyed by a kamikaze.

The rest of Taylor's service was spent stateside. He spent time with his squadron living in Anaheim and helping train younger pilots. By the time the war was over, Taylor had earned enough points to leave the Navy thanks to his Navy Air Medal and two Distinguished Flying Crosses. He retired in part due to the danger of flying the new jets the Navy was pushing, joining the reserves for two years before resigning his commission before the Korean War. Tallying up his experiences as a pilot, Taylor counted "about thirty-two to thirty-five combat [flights], where I actually went out and attacked an island or got into a melee," and eighty-two carrier landings totaling up to 1,000 flight hours, including his time in training.[445]

Returning to civilian life, Taylor moved back home to St. Louis to start a family with his wife. He started a small trucking business, but quickly moved on to work at a Cadillac distributorship in 1948, where he worked his way up to becoming a sales manager.[446] Coming from the military, Taylor had little ambition in business, until he began to notice the fact that cars leased by a Greyhound subsidiary were becoming more common on the streets of St. Louis.[447] In 1957, he took his first step into

---

[444] Winkler, David F. "NHF Oral History Program | LT Jack C. Taylor," September 2001. https://www.navyhistory.org/wp-content/uploads/2011/04/Jack-Taylor-Oral-History.pdf.

[445] Winkler, David F. "NHF Oral History Program | LT Jack C. Taylor," September 2001. https://www.navyhistory.org/wp-content/uploads/2011/04/Jack-Taylor-Oral-History.pdf.

[446] "Washington University in St. Louis Magazine," August 1, 2010. https://web.archive.org/web/20100801183837/http://magazine.wustl.edu/Summer03/mywashington.html.

[447] Smith, Harrison. "Jack C. Taylor, Founder of Rental-Car Giant Enterprise, Dies at 94." *Washington Post*, July 5, 2016, sec. Business. https://www.washingtonpost.com/business/jack-c-taylor-founder-of-rental-car-giant-enterprise-dies-at-94/2016/07/05/748bc16a-42b8-11e6-bc99-7d269f8719b1_story.html.

entrepreneurship, deciding to join the leasing industry. With the help of the dealership owner, Arthur Lindburg, he set up a car leasing business operating out of the lower level of the dealership where he worked, putting up 50% of his pay and $25,000 of his own money.[448,449] The company, at first named Executive Leasing, started small, with just one employee and seven cars to work with. His main customers were actually customers of the dealership whose cars were in the shop for repairs.[450]

According to Taylor's son, "In the early stages, when many car rental companies were focused on airports, my father explored a different path. He heard from customers [that] they wanted to rent cars where they live and work, not just at airports. He listened to this feedback and built an unparalleled neighborhood network of Enterprise Rent-A-Car locations in communities across North America and eventually Western Europe."[451] This business model would eventually become known as the "home city" car rental market, allowing customers access to cars on-demand from more convenient neighborhood locations. The industry would one day grow to be just as large as the airport leasing segment, with Taylor leading the way.[452]

---

[448] ehi.com. "Heritage." Accessed June 15, 2022.
https://www.enterpriseholdings.com/en/global-leadership/Heritage.html.

[449] The Curators of the University of Missouri. "Jack C. Taylor, Enterprise Rent-A-Car," 2009.
http://mohistory.umsl.edu/PDF/TAYLOR-Student.pdf.

[450] Chicago Tribune. "Enterprise Rent-A-Car Founder Jack Taylor Dies at 94." Accessed June 15, 2022.
https://www.chicagotribune.com/business/ct-enterprise-founder-jack-taylor-dies-20160702-story.html.

[451] National Defense Transportation Association. "Enterprising Ideas: An Interview with Andy Taylor and Bryan Scott of Enterprise Holdings," January 7, 2020.
https://www.ndtahq.com/enterprising-ideas-an-interview-with-andy-taylor-and-bryan-scott-of-enterprise-holdings/.

[452] St. Louis Business Journal. "Obituary of Jack Taylor, Founder of Enterprise Rent-A-Car." Accessed June 15, 2022.
https://www.bizjournals.com/stlouis/news/2016/07/02/jack-taylor-obituary.html.

While the idea behind Executive Leasing would one day become a billion-dollar industry, the company grew slowly at first. Taylor only recorded his first profit three years into the business, with the fleet growing to 1,000 cars and three St. Louis locations by 1961.[453] He often went above and beyond for his customers, fully embodying his famous quote: "Take care of your customers and employees first, and the profits will follow."[454] When some good customers asked for shorter-term leases than he would normally provide, Taylor would sometimes give in to their requests, handing over the keys despite not wanting to get into the rental-car business, which he viewed as both cutthroat and too time-consuming for his employees. By 1963, though, he eventually caved to the idea, building a fleet of 17 Chevies which he rented out for $5 a day and 5 cents a mile.[455]

In 1969, Taylor decided to take his business to the next level. He expanded outside of St. Louis and also rebranded, changing the company's name from Executive Leasing to Enterprise, in honor of the aircraft carrier he served on during World War 2. A few factors contributed to the name change, according to Taylor: "There was already an Executive Leasing Company in Atlanta. So we said we have to get another name in Atlanta. Because we have the 'E' logo, we want it to start with an 'E.' We were thinking about 'Essex.' But 'Essex' is kind of a ponderous name. So then we thought: I was on the Enterprise; let's think about 'Enterprise.' So we started talking about the

---

[453] Jr, Robert D. Hershey. "Jack Taylor, Founder of Enterprise Rent-A-Car, Dies at 94." *The New York Times*, July 3, 2016, sec. Business.
https://www.nytimes.com/2016/07/03/business/jack-taylor-founder-of-enterprise-rent-a-car-dies-at-94.html
[454] ehi.com. "Jack Crawford Taylor: War Hero, Business Leader, Philanthropist." Accessed June 17, 2022.
https://www.enterpriseholdings.com/en/press-archive/2016/07/jack-crawford-taylor-war-hero-business-leader-philanthropist.html.
[455] Jr, Robert D. Hershey. "Jack Taylor, Founder of Enterprise Rent-A-Car, Dies at 94." *The New York Times*, July 3, 2016, sec. Business.
https://www.nytimes.com/2016/07/03/business/jack-taylor-founder-of-enterprise-rent-a-car-dies-at-94.html

name 'Enterprise,' and 'Enterprise' has an upbeat, go-go, positive image. So we went to 'Enterprise.' And that's how we got the name. Because we had the 'E.' And when I name things, I try to name them where there's some sentimental attachment."[456]

The business continued to expand across the U.S., reaching a fleet size of 6,000 cars by 1980 with a focus on urban areas. The company expanded its services based on customer feedback, including airport rental services and even giving out free rides to its rental offices. Continuing Enterprise's focus on customer service, Taylor set up a "customer giveaway account" to allow managers to cut prices for difficult customers and created a promotion system aimed at ensuring accountability from the company's new hires.[457]

In 1980, Taylor's younger brother Paul joined the company, coming to Enterprise with years of experience in the automotive owning and leasing industry.[458] At Enterprise, he led the company in a series of mergers and acquisitions which allowed the company to expand nationwide, also helping establish more efficient vehicle disposal systems to cycle out older cars from the company's fleet. Keeping the business in the family, Taylor's son Andrew C. Taylor also worked for Enterprise, starting as a car washer at the age of 16 before becoming General Manager of the St. Louis region in 1976. He is now the executive chairman of Enterprise holdings, the parent company of Enterprise Rent-A-Car. Andrew's sister, Jo Ann Taylor Kindle, is the president of the Enterprise Holdings Foundation, the company's foundation focused on making philanthropic

---

[456] Winkler, David F. "NHF Oral History Program | LT Jack C. Taylor," September 2001. https://www.navyhistory.org/wp-content/uploads/2011/04/Jack-Taylor-Oral-History.pdf.

[457] Smith, Harrison. "Jack C. Taylor, Founder of Rental-Car Giant Enterprise, Dies at 94." *Washington Post*, July 5, 2016, sec. Business. https://www.washingtonpost.com/business/jack-c-taylor-founder-of-rental-car-giant-enterprise-dies-at-94/2016/07/05/748bc16a-42b8-11e6-bc99-7d269f8719b1_story.html.

[458] archive.ph. "Paul Taylor: Helped Brother Build Enterprise Leasing, the Nation's La...," April 15, 2013. https://archive.ph/iGybF.

donations to nonprofit organizations.[459] With the company settling in as one of the major automobile leasing businesses in the U.S. with growing international presence, Jack Taylor stepped down as CEO in 1991 (appointing his son to the position), and left his seat as executive chairman in 2013.[460] Today, Enterprise Rent-A-Car is the largest global car rental network, with 9,500 car rental locations in almost 100 countries. Enterprise Holdings, the business' parent company, also owns Alamo Rent a Car and National Car Rental, which it acquired in 2007. In 2021, Enterprise Holdings had a total revenue of $23.9 billion, with a fleet of over 1.85 million cars and trucks.

Post-retirement from Enterprise, Jack Taylor spent his time quietly giving money to charitable organizations around the world – the company estimated his donations totaled $860 million since 1982 – with a focus on environmental initiatives as well as giving back in the St. Louis area.[461] "I've just got more money than I need," he noted in an interview, "and there are people out there that don't have as much as they need to have for a reasonably happy life, and I give them some of mine."[462] Honoring Taylor's love of philanthropy, Enterprise continues to give back to communities to this day through the Enterprise Holdings Foundation. The Foundation donated $57.7 million in

---

[459] Jr, Robert D. Hershey. "Jack Taylor, Founder of Enterprise Rent-A-Car, Dies at 94." *The New York Times*, July 3, 2016, sec. Business. https://www.nytimes.com/2016/07/03/business/jack-taylor-founder-of-enterprise-rent-a-car-dies-at-94.html
[460] Chicago Tribune. "Enterprise Rent-A-Car Founder Jack Taylor Dies at 94." Accessed June 15, 2022. https://www.chicagotribune.com/business/ct-enterprise-founder-jack-taylor-dies-20160702-story.html.
[461] Smith, Harrison. "Jack C. Taylor, Founder of Rental-Car Giant Enterprise, Dies at 94." *Washington Post*, July 5, 2016, sec. Business. https://www.washingtonpost.com/business/jack-c-taylor-founder-of-rental-car-giant-enterprise-dies-at-94/2016/07/05/748bc16a-42b8-11e6-bc99-7d269f8719b1_story.html.
[462] Mail Online. "Enterprise Shares Video in Remembrance of Founder Jack Taylor | Daily Mail Online." Accessed July 1, 2022. http://www.dailymail.co.uk/video/news/video-1304331/Enterprise-shares-video-remembrance-founder-Jack-Taylor.html.

2021, 98% of which went to nonprofits requested by employees, helping uplift the communities of the people who make up the company.[463] Looking back on his life, Taylor had reflected, "I have had a beautiful life – health-wise, money-wise, family-wise, kid-wise. You know, it's almost too good to be true."[464] Taylor passed away on July 2, 2016, at the age of 94 of an unspecified illness.[465]

---

[463] ehi.com. "Enterprise Holdings Foundation." Accessed July 1, 2022. https://www.enterpriseholdings.com/en/corporate-social-responsibility/enterprise-holdings-foundation.html

[464] Mail Online. "Enterprise Shares Video in Remembrance of Founder Jack Taylor | Daily Mail Online." Accessed July 1, 2022. http://www.dailymail.co.uk/video/news/video-1304331/Enterprise-shares-video-remembrance-founder-Jack-Taylor.html.

[465] Smith, Harrison. "Jack C. Taylor, Founder of Rental-Car Giant Enterprise, Dies at 94." *Washington Post*, July 5, 2016, sec. Business. https://www.washingtonpost.com/business/jack-c-taylor-founder-of-rental-car-giant-enterprise-dies-at-94/2016/07/05/748bc16a-42b8-11e6-bc99-7d269f8719b1_story.html.

XVII.

Chuck Wallace

U.S. Air Force

Esurance

Charles "Chuck" Wallace was born in 1964, in the rural town of Hebron, Connecticut. He attended East Catholic High School in Manchester, Connecticut, graduating with the class of 1982.[466] During his high school years, Wallace picked up an interest in aviation and space, in part due to the U.S. government's focus on space programs as he grew up. As his two older sisters headed off to college, Wallace realized he needed to pick a direction in life and eventually decided he wanted to become a pilot. With his parents' support, he talked to some pilots to figure out how to fulfill his goals, and they pointed him to the military as the best place to start a career as a pilot.

Wallace focused his efforts on getting into the United States Air Force Academy, which he was told was the guaranteed way to become a military pilot, and also earned his private pilot's license as a high schooler. "I worked my ass off to get in [to the Academy], and I barely got in," he recalls. "I got accepted in May, part of the last wave to get accepted." Following graduation, he headed straight to the Air Force Academy, where he earned a Bachelors of Engineering in Engineering Mechanics in 1986. While he was a disciplined student, Wallace remembers, "I found myself in a lot of hot water at the Academy because I was a little more independent-minded."

After graduating from the Academy, Wallace went to Reese Air Force Base in Lubbock, Texas, where he helped train future jet pilots to earn their wings.[467] In 1991, he headed overseas to the Rhein-Main Airbase in Frankfurt, Germany, where he served as a C-130 Hercules Aircraft Commander, leading his aircraft on missions to Europe, Africa, and Asia.[468] In Germany, he also served as an advisor to the Wing Commander,

---

[466] "Education | Chuck Wallace | LinkedIn." Accessed September 2, 2022. https://www.linkedin.com/in/chuckwallace/details/education/.
[467] Clearsurance. "Esurance Co-Founder and Former Senior Executive Chuck Wallace Joins Clearsurance Board of Directors." Accessed September 2, 2022. https://clearsurance.com/blog/esurance-co-founder-and-former-senior-executive-chuck-wallace-joins.
[468] "Experience | Chuck Wallace | LinkedIn." Accessed March 16, 2023. https://www.linkedin.com/in/chuckwallace/details/experience/.

helping set up the execution of Operation Provide Promise, a humanitarian relief operation to Bosnia and Herzegovina that took place during the Yugoslav Wars. It was the longest running humanitarian airlift in history, with 21 countries dropping over 100,000 tons of supplies into Sarajevo as the city came under siege by the Yugoslav People's Army and the Army of Republika Srpska. Despite the laundry list of achievements, after 4 years of active duty, Wallace realized that he didn't actually want to be an Air Force man for the rest of his life, and instead chose to head back to civilian life and pursue a career in law.

He left active duty in Germany in 1993, heading back stateside and joining the Air Force Reserves to fly C-130s. During this time, he applied to all 11 law schools located near C-130 bases across the country. He ended up on the waitlist at the University of Pennsylvania's law school, and eventually got accepted as a full-time student after paying a couple of visits to plead his case at the admissions office. During his first year in law school, Wallace realized that he'd also fit in at UPenn's Wharton School of Business, and applied there as well. While his first application was rejected, Wallace re-applied in his second year and was eventually accepted, after he again paid a few visits to the admissions office. To clarify, his second application was on the borderline of acceptance to the Wharton School, and his tenacity secured his spot. Wallace graduated from both schools in 1997, earning a JD in Business and Corporate Law from UPenn's Carey Law School and an MBA in Business & Emerging Technologies from the Wharton School. After finishing his higher education in Pennsylvania, Wallace turned back to the Air Force for a time, working as a Judge Advocate Officer at Andrews Air Force Base in Maryland while simultaneously working at Remote Source Lighting International, a mass-lighting company, as Director of International Business Development.[469]

Riding the dot-com wave of the late 90s, Wallace headed out west to California to sleep on a fellow Air Force Academy

---

[469] "Experience | Chuck Wallace | LinkedIn." Accessed March 16, 2023. https://www.linkedin.com/in/chuckwallace/details/experience/.

grad's couch. There, he searched for opportunities, eventually linking up with four other Wharton grads to co-found Esurance. "In the dot-com days when we started Esurance, there was no infrastructure or environment supporting InsurTech innovation to speak of, other than a general enthusiasm for any company that was addressing innovation in a large consumer market, regardless of the industry," he remembers. "The general approach to company building in the dot-com era was often focused on how much money could be raised over multiple rounds of funding, how fast a company could launch and then quickly expand into new markets, and how quickly a company could get to an IPO if it didn't get acquired along the way. The general sentiment was that companies with momentum (regardless of the long-term viability of their underlying business model) could also get a substantial next round of funding on their way to an IPO. And then post-IPO could fix any issues with the underlying business on the way to self-sustaining profitability and long term growth."[470]

The sector that Esurance wanted to push into using the power of the internet was the insurance market, looking to beat industry giants like State Farm, Allstate, Progressive, and GEICO by growing through their online presence. While other dot-com era insurance ventures were simply working as direct-to-consumer marketplaces or insurance sales agencies, Esurance was one of the first to build out a full, risk-bearing insurance provider online.

Wallace worked at multiple positions for his company, including Information Security Officer, General Counsel, and Vice President of Business Development. After 18 months at the company, he was the only founder left. As Information Security officer, Wallace helped set up and manage security and privacy systems, with no major security breaches occurring during his time in the position. As General Counsel, he directed legal and

---

[470] CB Insights Research. "Insurance Tech in the Dot-Com Bubble: Lessons from Esurance & ECoverage," November 9, 2016. https://www.cbinsights.com/research/insurance-tech-dot-com-bubble/
.

regulatory teams, managing litigation at various levels of the business. Finally, as Vice President of Business Development, he expanded the business' customer base while also acquiring new business partners for the company to work with.

While working at Esurance, Wallace was able to draw many parallels between his time in the military and his time guiding his first early-stage company to success. "I think there is a strong parallel between my experience in the military and what it's like to be in an early stage company," he said. "When you're in an operating role in the military, say you're a platoon leader or in a platoon, you're in a small group of people but you have a certain amount of structure around you – the military structure, the rules of engagement, and things like that. Within that, it's a very autonomous small group where you have to rely on each other for your success and there's nobody else that's going to make you successful. It's very much the same when you're flying a C-130 in the middle of Africa somewhere, far away from the structure of the military. You have to go out and get the mission done, and you have to rely on each other for your success. It's just like that at a small company, where you again have a very small group of people and you're either going to make it successful by what you to accomplish together or you're not, and there's no bureaucracy of a big company that just keeps things chugging along, whether the small or big initiatives do well or not. And so that same dynamic of small, highly dedicated teams that rely on each other for everything goes across both experiences. And that's what I enjoy so much about company building – you have that dynamic, and it helps you realize that you've got to get stuff done, you've got to rely on other people, you've got to plan well and execute well or else it's just not going to happen."

"In both environments, there are three things you've got to be able to do well. You need to be able to think strategically, understanding the strategic weave and the thread of things that are going on because those inform a lot of smaller decisions; you need to be able to execute tactically, meaning you have to be able to take on higher-level strategy whether you thought of it yourself or you're taking on someone else's strategy, and actually make things happen; and you have to be able to build and operate within a team. Think strategically, execute tactically, build and lead a team. It takes all three."

During his time with Esurance, the company grew to expand its revenue from $3.5 million in 2000 to $201 million in 2005. Esurance was one of the few dot-com companies to hit a slight growth period after the bubble burst in 2000, thanks to financial help from White Mountains Insurance Group. Wallace left the company in 2007 as its premiums reached $1 billion. It was sold to Allstate for $1 billion in 2011.[471]

Over the next few years, Wallace worked at various tech companies. He joined Ustream.tv (a video streaming platform) as CEO before becoming president of uSell, an online recommerce site. From there, he worked as Vice President of Operations at Automatic Labs, an app-based vehicle assistance company, before returning to the world of insurance with High Definition Vehicle Insurance, where he currently works as co-founder and CEO. He believes that the company is uniquely positioned for the future, at the intersection of three markets which each have room to grow: insurance, freight and logistics, and mobility. The company seeks to improve the process of commercial vehicle insurance for trucking fleets.

---

[471] CB Insights Research. "Insurance Tech in the Dot-Com Bubble: Lessons from Esurance & ECoverage," November 9, 2016. https://www.cbinsights.com/research/insurance-tech-dot-com-bubble/

XIII.
Dave Liniger

U.S. Air Force

RE/MAX

Dave Liniger was born on Sept. 25, 1945 in the small town of Marion, Indiana. His parents owned a 10-acre family farm and a small business in town, and he grew up a relatively average Midwestern boy, participating in the Cub Scouts and 4-H, another youth group organization. Growing up craving adventure, he told his parents, "The day I'm eighteen, I'm out of here."[472] Liniger started school early at the age of five and was an intelligent kid, if a bit immature. He loved to read and would easily understand key concepts from every book he consumed. Unfortunately for his grades, he did not want to consume his school textbooks. Liniger mainly earned Cs throughout his education, only snagging the occasional A when a subject piqued his interest enough for him to study it. While he lacked the discipline for school, Liniger knew he wanted to be rich. He worked many different odd jobs from a young age, knowing money was a guaranteed path to a more interesting life. Unfortunately, his entrepreneurial energy lacked a solid direction at this stage in his life.

For a while, Liniger continued his doomed relationship with education. As he'd started grade school early, he graduated high school a year early and headed to university. With even fewer constraints keeping him on track in college than in high school and no self-discipline built up, he floundered and fell behind his peers quickly. After his first semester, Liniger was put on academic probation but vowed to be a better student after the break. He succeeded for a period before falling back into his old ways. He realized that he lacked a goal – while other kids were studying to become doctors or lawyers, the only thing he desired was some amorphous definition of success in the business world. He dropped out, moving back home to help with his father's blue-collar business.

Doing physical labor took its toll on Liniger – he considered his job humiliating and low class, but also envied the passion some of his father's other employees showed for their

---

[472] Harkins, P., Hollihan, K., & Liniger, D. (2007). *Everybody Wins: The Story and Lessons Behind RE/MAX* (1st edition). Wiley.

jobs. Looking for adventure, he ended up meeting a girl and got her pregnant. He applied for the Air Force in 1968 in the hopes of providing for his young family in a more "glamorous" way. Liniger had initially applied as a paramedic, but the Air Force simply needed bodies at this point in the Vietnam War, so he only completed basic training before being shipped overseas. While obviously Vietnam was no walk in the park for anyone involved, the change of scenery satisfied Liniger's thirst for adventure. He was so invigorated in Vietnam that at one point, he wrote home to his parents, jokingly saying that no matter how bad things seemed in the news, Vietnam was definitely a better place than Indiana. "The military really gave me the chance to grow up," he remembers of his service. "It was fun. I thought it was a fabulous place. If I could have become an officer or made any kind of living at all, I would have stayed with it. I loved the camaraderie and being around airplanes and tanks and guns and the adventure of it all. It also taught me self-discipline and a sense of responsibility. I married young, had children and grew up very quickly, knowing I had to make a living for these kids."[473]

Just before he deployed to Vietnam, Liniger had taken a key step in his life's journey. Combining the base pay from the Air Force with the money from his three part-time jobs, he was able to buy a house for $10,450, fixing it up and selling it for $4,000 in profit.[474] The house's sale earned him almost as much as the yearly wages for all four of his day jobs combined. At the time, he was also reading a book by a former postman describing his rise from rags to riches. The author started his real estate career by buying a run-down property which he flipped for a profit, slowly buying more and more valuable properties before becoming a millionaire. Now, Liniger finally had a goal and a road map: he would return from Vietnam in one piece and make his fortune in the real estate business.

---

[473] Sharing the Dream: Dave Liniger of RE/MAX. (2005, February 1). *Airport Journals*.
http://airportjournals.com/sharing-the-dream-dave-liniger-of-remax/
[474] Harkins, P., Hollihan, K., & Liniger, D. (2007). *Everybody Wins: The Story and Lessons Behind RE/MAX* (1st edition). Wiley.

After returning to the States from Vietnam, Liniger took a job at Arizona State University with an ROTC detachment located at the school. The job was so easy that he began working on his plan even before his time with the Air Force was up. He sold 10 other officers on the promise of real estate profits, raising $1,000 from each while getting his own one-eleventh stake in the deal for free. The group, led by Liniger, bought and flipped a house, earning themselves 200% profits on the sale. Continuing down his shining path to riches, he earned his real estate license and joined a company named Ed Thirkhill Realty, looking to put his youthful vigor to work in a booming industry. With Mr. Thirkill, over a period of six months, Liniger failed spectacularly. He could not find a single seller and thus landed a grand total of zero sales in half a year. He gave up on his dream, at least temporarily.

If he hadn't already paid $20 for a ticket to see a real estate motivational speaker, real estate giant and disruptor RE/MAX would never have existed. Because he'd already sent the money to attend the talk by Dave Stone, Dave Liniger dragged his defeated self to the Mountain Shadow Country Club in Phoenix, plopping himself down in a front row seat. At the talk, he found his passion for real estate reignited. Speaking to Stone after the talk, he told his new idol that if he could just speak like him, Liniger could become the real estate mogul he knew he could be. He then revealed his six-month dry spell to Stone, who promptly told him to quit the business. Taking this as a reverse-psychology motivation attempt, Liniger felt himself reinvigorated to sell houses.

Later that very same day, Liniger ran into a young woman speaking to her grandfather in Spanish at the grocery store. Using his limited knowledge of the language, he gathered that they were talking about selling the older man's house. Liniger jumped into the conversation, offering himself as an agent. The next day, he took a look at the house – a fixer-upper, which he felt comfortable he could sell for a guaranteed profit. He listed it, and the property sold for full price that night. Heading to bed, he told his wife, "Honey, you're sleeping with one hell of a fine real estate agent. Do you realize that 100 percent of my listings have sold for 100 percent of the price in one hour or less?"[475] From that first success, Liniger went on to sell three more houses soon after, helping the granddaughter and her fiancé land a new place and using their referrals to sell two more houses. He ended his six-month dry spell with four sales in 48 hours, with another listing in his pocket.

Liniger's success continued as he attached himself at the hip to Dave Stone, following him around from lecture to lecture and taking every course possible. His newfound charisma and ability to sell began lining his pockets, leading to a new car and a salesman-of-the-month plaque. He soon moved on from Ed Thirkill Realty, finding similar success in a larger company named Realty Executives. The company had an interesting structure where agents simply paid a fee to work under the company, keeping 100% of commissions past that fee. While others disparaged it as a "rent-a-desk" operation, he enjoyed the freedom.

He was able to easily fund his growing young family by this point, and took another chance after a short period at Realty Executives, moving the gang to Denver, Colorado and finding a position at Van Schaack and Company, a highly professional top real estate firm in the area. At this point, Liniger had found his rhythm, quickly shooting to the top of the real estate food chain in Denver as well. Now that he'd reached the top, he knew that success as an agent was not the endgame he was looking for. Clients trusted and bought houses from him as a person, not the Van Schaack company name. He understood that the company played an important role in the business structure, but felt that agents got the short end of the stick in terms of return for their efforts.

So, Liniger decided to go about setting up his own company. Looking back on his experiences at different real estate companies, he realized that he didn't have to choose between the

---

[475] Harkins, P., Hollihan, K., & Liniger, D. (2007). *Everybody Wins: The Story and Lessons Behind RE/MAX* (1st edition). Wiley.

professional rigidity of Van Schaack or the loose "rent-a-desk" structure of Realty Executives. Instead, he could make a hybrid of the two – his company would combine the reputation and support systems of Van Schaack with the looser structure and performance-based empowerment of Realty Executives. With better training methods alongside increased financial motivation, agents would be able to flourish in their careers. The more professional support systems offered by the company would present a more stable image to customers as well. He felt that this new concept for real estate company structure could be a smash hit and even scale to become an international powerhouse. After spending just one year with Van Schaack, Liniger left the company to bet on his own idea.

In January of 1973, his experiment began in earnest. A land development firm named Weydert reached out to Liniger asking for him to come on board as a sales manager, but he declined the position before returning with a counteroffer. He told Jim Collins, the Weydert representative, that he was planning to build his own unique real estate company. Weydert was looking to expand, so Liniger's plan for a scaling real estate network sounded right up their alley. Luckily for Liniger, his very first business pitch worked out for him, and Weydert signed him on, promising him one-fifth of the company in exchange for four-fifths of the company Liniger was looking to create. After thinking about it for a bit, the young entrepreneur decided to sign on. He felt connected to Weydert's investors (who were all veterans), and also realized that the company's capital and experience would go a long way for his fledgling company.

But first, that fledgling company needed a name. Liniger's first meeting with Weydert involved a bottle of tequila and the name "Real Estate Maximums Incorporated." Everyone involved liked the name, specifically its reference to "maximums," meaning that both customers and agents would get the most from the company, as well its "everyone wins" message. The name felt a bit too long, however, so the meeting continued in search of a shorter name. "R.E. Max" was thrown around but felt too similar to a real person's name. Inspired by Exxon's branding and its use of an "X" with a slash through it, Liniger jotted out the name "RE/MAX" on a piece of paper. It stuck.

Unfortunately, the shiny new name would be the last good news Liniger would have for a while. While Weydert had promised him hundreds of thousands of dollars in starting capital, the group was highly leveraged in a bad economy as RE/MAX stepped out into the world. The group could only spare Liniger $15,000, which he used to secure office space and start searching for employees. His most important investment at this stage was an administrative assistant named Gail Main, who would end up co-leading RE/MAX further down the line. She saw the potential in the logic of Liniger's idea and wanted to stick around to see if he could truly build it into the massive company that he promised.

With his assistant running day-to-day operations, Liniger turned to hiring new agents. He put out an ad in the Denver Post that read, "Why split your commissions when you can keep the whole thing yourself?" His office received over a thousand applications, leading to 204 recruitment attempts and eventually four RE/MAX agents hired. All four were hired for two reasons: their hunger for success and their belief in the RE/MAX system. The kicker? In a world where female real estate agents faced a very real glass ceiling, three out of four of Liniger's first hires were women.

"It started as a very basic real estate company here in Englewood," Liniger says of the company's start. "It grew to eight offices and we were number one in Denver by 1978, but it was a tough beginning. We didn't have enough finances, our backers dropped out and the industry never wanted to see the thing succeed." The company made up for their lack of support with hard work. The first 50 employees were all selected for their hunger and enthusiasm for the concept behind RE/MAX, and worked long days to get the company off the ground. They were grinding out 12 hour days, seven days a week, and anyone who got into the office after 6:30 am was considered a straggler. By 1975, the company established its first franchise outside of Colorado, reaching 100 franchises by 1977.

At the time, the real estate brokerage landscape looked like a cottage industry compared to today. In 1973, less than 12 real estate firms had more than 200 agents under their wings. Most were mom-and-pop companies with a handful of agents, many of whom were only involved in the industry as part-timers. Perhaps the biggest sign of the industry's old-time sensibilities was the National Association of Realtors (NAR) "Code of Ethics," based around its "Golden Rule": "Do unto others as you would have them do unto you." One important example of this was the Code of Ethics' Article 24: "Thou shalt not solicit agents from another broker." RE/MAX's hiring strategies directly opposed this, with their ads questioning why an agent would split their commissions with their broker. As RE/MAX found more success, many local Boards of Realtors dragged Liniger into meetings for his violations of Article 24. At one point, he snapped. "I want you to know," he said, "that what you're doing here today is hindering free commerce. That's antitrust activity, and anybody who violates antitrust goes to jail. I didn't fight in Vietnam to listen to you tell me I can't offer your agent another job at a higher wage. I'm going to file criminal charges against you, and I refuse to participate any further in these meetings because doing so makes me a co-conspirator in your price-fixing activities."[476] The threat worked, even though Liniger had no attorney at the time. The NAR and other real estate bodies were facing down extensive antitrust suits from the federal government at the time, so the threat of further legal action (with no actual substance) scared them into abolishing Article 24.

From there, RE/MAX continued to expand nationwide, opening offices and selling franchises based on the strength of the company's concept as well as its growing network of support. The company also developed a new strategy, thanks to the abolishment of Article 24: poaching top agents in a region. This practice came into play after some analysis by Liniger. He found that the top 20% of all agents in a region were responsible for

---

[476] Harkins, P., Hollihan, K., & Liniger, D. (2007). *Everybody Wins: The Story and Lessons Behind RE/MAX* (1st edition). Wiley.

roughly 30-40% of the real estate market share in that region. The company invested in these agents, disregarding the short-term costs with an eye on long-term growth.

By 1983, RE/MAX began really hitting its stride. The American real estate market took off during the 80s, with companies like Century 21 going public and Sears dipping its toes in the game. Despite the moves of other firms, RE/MAX reached the top of the market in 1983, becoming the number one real estate company in the nation based on real estate sold. Other companies began shifting towards the agent-favored RE/MAX model, experimenting with 75/25 or 80/20 splits instead of the usual 50/50 profit share between firm and agent.

Local players also began consolidating under larger firms, especially Hospitality Franchise Systems, which owned Coldwell Banker, Century 21, and ERA. Luckily, RE/MAX's focus on top agent efficiency began paying off this time, helping it remain the top real estate firm by 2003. In 1981, the company went international in Canada, and by 1994 RE/MAX had expanded overseas with RE/MAX Europe. By 2006, RE/MAX expanded its online presence and by 2009 it had franchises in 70 countries worldwide. The company went public in 2013, gathering $220 million for its IPO and $185 million for its second public offering in 2015, when it earned revenues of $177 million.

Liniger retired as CEO in 2018, though he is still involved in the company as Chairman of the RE/MAX Board. In 2012, he fought through a life-threatening staph infection which lead to total organ failure and a flat-line before doctors put him into a four-week drug-induced coma.[477] His mobility remains limited today thanks to the infection, but he is continuing to recover mentally and physically. Outside the operating and board rooms, Liniger still remains active. He owns The Wildlife Experience, a conservation facility in Denver, and also donates to national and local charities.

---

[477] *Dave Liniger*. (n.d.). Retrieved September 23, 2022, from //www.daveliniger.com/

Tim Hsia is a distinguished honor graduate of West Point and was commissioned as an infantry officer in the US Army. Tim deployed twice to Iraq: he served as an infantry platoon leader in combat with 1-24 Infantry, 1st Brigade, 25th Infantry Division in Mosul, Iraq. As an executive officer with 3rd Squadron, 2nd Stryker Cavalry Regiment (3/2 SCR) he helped the unit move from Ft. Lewis, WA to Vilseck, Germany. He then served as a logistics officer for 3/2 SCR during its fourteen month deployment in support of the surge in Iraq and earned a Bronze Star.

Tim transitioned from active duty in 2010 and graduated from Stanford's Graduate School of Business and Stanford Law School in 2014. While at Stanford he taught ROTC to cadets at Stanford and Santa Clara University.

Tim is the CEO & Founder of Media Mobilize (an online ad network, marketing agency, and media company).

Tim is the founder and Managing Partner of Context Ventures, a venture fund that invests in military veteran founders and also in consumer startups. Tim's startup investments prior to Context Ventures include Workflow (acquired by Apple), Morning Brew (acquired by Business Insider), The Hustle (acquired by HubSpot), Thredup (IPO), Proterra (SPAC), Bright Cellars, FabFitFun, Verb Energy, Lime (scooter), and Secureframe.

Tim is a board member at Service to School (co-founder), Bunker Labs, and the Marine's Memorial

Association (Marine Memorial Club and Hotel in San Francisco). He is also a Pat Tillman Foundation Scholar.

Tim is a published writer in the Infantry Magazine, Small Wars Journal, The Los Angeles Times, and The New York Times (two op-eds and first military writer for the New York Times At War blog).

Tim and his family live and work in San Francisco. He enjoys running, reading, and spending time with his family.

Marcus Gee-Lim is a writer currently based in San Francisco. He's worked on projects including the *Best American Nonrequired Reading* anthology series, and also writes for the Daily Pnut, an email newsletter. He enjoys cooking, hiking, and learning new things.

Made in the USA
Monee, IL
30 October 2023